The Morning I Walked Her Home

By

Shelley Fraser

The Morning I Walked Her Home

Dedication

For Sister John

In memory of the woman who entered my life at an early age and whose quiet guidance and steady belief helped make me the person I am today. She encouraged me to do great things, and her words still stay with me, reminding me to continue forward even when the path was difficult. Our connection was personal, private, and deeply formative, and its imprint remains with me still. Thank you for seeing me, guiding me, and believing in me when I needed it most.

Acknowledgements

To Bev and Marlene, I extend my sincere appreciation for your creativity and for your contributions to the development of the book cover.

To my students, past and present, your curiosity and resilience have continually reminded me that learning is a shared and evolving journey.

My gratitude is also extended to my cousins Sonya and Julie, to my former Biology teacher and cherished friend Ruth, and to the many friends whose kindness and steady presence offered strength during challenging times.

I am profoundly grateful to Sister John's family for reaching out with such thoughtfulness and care.

To all who grieve the loss of someone dear, please know that you are not alone. Though your loved one has left this world, their presence endures in memory and in love. May you find comfort in remembrance and hope in the enduring truth that love does not fade.

With gratitude

Shelley Fraser

Table of Contents

Prologue

Every life is shaped by the people who walk beside us. Some stay only for a moment, and others remain for a lifetime.

I never imagined that a Catholic sister would become one of the most defining relationships of my life, or that her presence would carry me through some of my darkest moments and help me grow in ways I never thought possible after coming from a broken home.

For more than forty-four years, our connection was a steady and grounding force that shaped not only who I was but who I would become. Life carried us down different paths, and for twelve or thirteen of those years we had no contact at all. Yet the bond between us never faded. It lived quietly inside me, unchanged by distance and untouched by silence.

When I finally returned to her, my reason was simple. I returned out of love. It was a love shaped by decades of knowing her, learning from her, and being quietly held by her presence, even in the years when we lived separate lives.

This memoir shares the story of that unlikely bond and the way two vastly different lives became intertwined. It explores how love can arrive in unexpected forms and how grief, even in its pain, can reveal the quiet strength we carry within us.

And in the end, when her final days drew near, everything we had shared gathered into a truth I could no longer ignore. That is where this story begins.

The End is Near

On December 14, 2024, I decided to gently sponge Sister John's mouth. I hesitated at first, unsure whether she would resist the way she often had with the caregivers. Leaning in, I whispered, "Please, Sister, I just want to help you stay hydrated. You haven't been drinking much, so please don't push me away." To my relief, she didn't.

I sat quietly beside her bed, letting the stillness of her care home room surround us. Slowly, I moistened her lips and watched her swallow with effort. Sometimes droplets slipped from the corners of her mouth, and she would instinctively reach for the bed sheet to wipe them. Each time, I gently intervened. "Sister, I will get that for you," I said, dabbing the water from her chin.

As I continued caring for her, I found myself sharing memories, moments we had lived together, stories that shaped both of us. It felt surreal tending to a woman who had always carried herself with such spiritual strength, now resting so vulnerably before me. Beneath the habit and the title, she was human. She was someone I loved deeply, someone who had shaped me in ways I could never fully articulate.

In that moment, the roles shifted. I was no longer the one being guided; I had become the one offering comfort. And it felt right. It felt sacred, as though we had reached the final page of a story written in compassion, trust, and grace.

In the days that followed, I realized this was a story that needed to be told. It was rare, profound, and deeply human. A story of two women whose lives had become inseparably woven together, one a Catholic sister whose presence offered a calm I had never known, the other a young girl searching for belonging, meaning, and light.

Our bond didn't fit a simple explanation, yet its impact was unmistakable. Together, we shaped each other in ways that left behind a legacy of love, resilience, and quiet transformation. It is a story that deserves to be remembered by anyone who understands the power of human connection.

Shelley Fraser

Chapter One
The Night I Chose to Stay

On the evening of December 15, 2024, I returned to Sister John's room, sensing that time was slipping away. As I entered, I noticed something I had not seen before; her mouth was slightly open, her eyes closed in a way that felt different. It startled me, and the reality of her condition settled deeper into my heart.

That night, I brought my computer to play music and chose songs filled with meaning, comfort, and memory. I played everything from "Wind Beneath My Wings" by Bette Midler to "The Dance" by Garth Brooks, along with Elvis Presley's gospel hymns. As the room filled with sound, I reached for Sister John's hand and held it, staying that way for hours.

I hesitated at first, aware of boundaries and of her role as a sister, but this was not a moment for protocol. Her time was near, and I needed her to know I was beside her. When I took her hand, I felt the faintest movement, her fingers gently wriggling against mine. I believe it was her quiet way of acknowledging me, as if to say, "I know you're here."

She never spoke that night. Eventually, I let go of her hand and told her softly, "I will be back shortly; I am going to speak to the nurse." I stepped out for about half an hour. When I returned, I immediately sensed a change in her breathing, a faint rattle that told me the end was close. Her eyes were open now. I alerted the staff, bracing myself for what was coming next.

A caregiver entered and said gently, "This does not sound good." She encouraged me to stay overnight and assured me more staff would be available in the morning. I agreed without hesitation. "I will stay with her," I said. "She is awake." Her breathing grew fainter by the minute. I stood beside her and whispered through tears, "This is really going to hurt…" Emotions rushed through me, years of memories, the bond we had built, all of it pressing in at once. I checked her breathing often, and at one point I thought she had passed. I called the nurse, who reassured me, "No, she is still breathing." But only a few moments later, her breath faded completely.

Sister John passed away shortly after 3:00 AM on December 16, 2024.

I informed the nurse, "I think you should call the sisters and let them know." She returned and gently covered Sister John with a blanket. I leaned forward and kissed her forehead. Then I sat in her reclining chair and whispered, "It's all over." I could hardly absorb what had just happened. Yet, in the middle of the shock, I felt an overwhelming sense of gratitude. Being with her during her final hours was a gift, an honor beyond anything words could express. The woman who had shaped me in so many ways was gone, and I could not imagine a more meaningful farewell.

The nurse told me the funeral home would not arrive until dawn. I said, "I will stay with her. I will not leave her alone." Waiting did not bother me. I wanted to be there until the very end.

When the funeral home staff arrived, they gently placed Sister John on the stretcher. I touched her shoulder and whispered softly, "You did a good job, Sister." They took her away quietly, before the other residents were up for breakfast. I remained in her room, sitting in silence, absorbing the weight of the moment.

Throughout the morning, caregivers stopped in to offer their condolences. I found myself talking about her, gesturing toward her bed as though she were still lying there. Her absence had not settled into my heart yet.

Around 8:00 AM, I left the care home and went straight to work. My coworkers were kind and urged me to go home and rest, but I could not be alone. I needed movement, people, noise, something to keep me going as I tried to process the loss. I closed my classroom door and sat there, thinking about those final hours and how they had compressed years of memories into a single night.

That night was not just an ending. It was the beginning of telling our story. I promised myself I would write it honestly and from the heart. What we shared never fit into simple categories. It held struggle, restraint, and pain, but also love and fear, the two most powerful forces that shape us.

In the end, it was something, call it loyalty, love, faithfulness, kindred spirits, or soul connection, that brought me back to her side.

Shelley Fraser

Chapter Two
Family Roots

My story began long before I understood it, shaped by the people who came before me.

My grandfather was a proud Scotsman from Edinburgh, his thick accent unmistakable. He had been married twice. His second wife, my grandmother, was from London and spoke with a strong English accent. Together, they settled in western Canada on the northern prairies of Saskatchewan, far from the worlds they once knew.

In the 1940s, my grandfather served in the Canadian Armed Forces. After the war, he and my grandmother built a life on a small farm near a French-speaking Catholic community called Hope, a place that would shape much of my early childhood. They had three children together, but tragedy struck early.

In 1951, my grandmother died of polio at just twenty-nine. My father was only four, with two younger sisters, and my grandfather suddenly found himself alone with three small children to raise.

On my mother's side, her heritage was Métis. Her parents spoke both French and English at home and were Catholic. She came from a large family of fourteen, nine brothers and five sisters.

In 1961, when she was ten, her mother died from complications related to asthma, and she and her sisters were moved between foster homes. Eventually, one family took in all the girls, which was a blessing, but the instability had already left its mark. My mother learned early to tuck her feelings away.

She attended school in Hope but often skipped class. The sisters would call her name and coax her back, sometimes gently and sometimes firmly. She would disappear with my dad, and they would drive off together, choosing escape over structure. Despite her chaotic upbringing, my mother had a generous heart and gave what she could, even when she had very little herself.

Years later, my grandfather moved into the community and proudly marched in annual parades, wearing his kilt to honor his Scottish heritage. Though both of my father's parents were Anglican, my parents decided to baptize their children as Roman Catholic, an early thread tying me to the Church long before I understood what faith meant.

My grandfather was very good to me. As his eldest grandchild, I often stayed at his house with his loyal gold and white border collie, Buster. He lived only a few houses away, and his home had more space, something I craved as I grew older. My parents' home was small and cramped, so I began dividing my time between both places. As I grew more aware, I noticed my grandfather's drinking worsening. I think he carried a sorrow he never spoke about, rooted in losing his wife so young.

The French Catholic community had a towering church and a two-story convent next door where the sisters lived. Though my parents were not churchgoers, I felt an unexplained pull toward the church from the age of six or seven. I began attending Sunday Mass alone.

In the early 1970s, the pews overflowed with large French-speaking families. Although I did not understand the language, I understood the feeling of belonging. I watched people line up for communion, studied their reverence, and noticed the sisters in their black and white habits. Sometimes my brother Stewart and I would see the sisters walking in pairs down our street, though we never spoke to them. Still, I loved going to school in that small community, where several Catholic sisters taught and created an atmosphere that felt safe to me.

When I look at those years, I can see that they were shaping me in ways I did not yet understand. My roots, my family's struggles, and the quiet comfort I found in the church were laying a foundation I couldn't yet see.

The Morning I Walked Her Home

Shelley Fraser

Chapter Three
The Year Everything Changed

In 1977, a season of change swept across many lives. That same year, the world lost Elvis Presley, whose light dimmed far too soon at forty-two.

In late June, my mother called from Calgary, Alberta. She asked me to bring some of her belongings. I was ten and did not know whether she was staying there for a short time or planning to live there, only that she needed me. She wanted me to take the Greyhound bus from Saskatchewan to Calgary.

My grandfather bought me a suitcase and a ticket, reminding me to ask for help during each transfer. I took three buses, watching the prairies pass in long, quiet stretches. When I arrived, my mother and Aunt Jenny were waiting at the depot.

I didn't know the full story behind my parents' marriage troubles until I asked, "Are we going back home?" She answered simply, "No, we're not." Those words shattered me. I didn't just lose my home; I lost my rhythm, my safety, and my sense of place. My father stayed behind with my two younger brothers, and suddenly nothing felt familiar.

Starting school in Calgary that fall was a struggle. The city felt overwhelming, and I experienced deep loneliness. My mother often neglected me, leaving me without food or supervision while she went out with friends for days at a time. I began missing school because no one was home to care for me. Eventually, a truant officer had to escort me. My first report card showed I had missed more than thirty days. Once the adults realized how neglected I truly was, social services began discussing the idea of sending me to Wood's Christian Home.

My grandfather didn't understand what was happening, and my father showed no concern. It was heartbreaking to feel so abandoned, as though I had slipped through the cracks of everyone's care.

The Morning I Walked Her Home

Years later, I would learn that while I was struggling to find my footing in Calgary in 1977, Sister John was studying in Rome. Our lives had not yet intersected, but we were already moving quietly toward the moment they finally would.

In 1978, I visited my aunt and uncle in Prince Albert. When they learned I hadn't been going to school, they brought me back to live with my grandfather. I eventually found my way back to school, but I carried a silent pain with me. I had been abused by neighbors on the street where I once lived, something I never spoke about, not to my mother, my father, or my grandfather, until I finally wrote about it years later. In those days, people did not talk about such things. Silence was the expectation.

When I entered grade five, I threw myself into sports such as soccer, floor hockey, and baseball, anything that demanded movement and focus. I was a strong player and was often chosen for teams. I loved our lunch hour games, especially watching the older girls who played with such confidence. I admired their leadership.

Sports became my refuge. On the field, I wasn't the girl who had been overlooked or left behind. I felt present, capable, and free. Each game gave me a sense of control, a place where I could belong without having to explain myself.

Something in me began to shift. Maybe it was resilience forming, or maybe it was simply the instinct to push forward despite everything. I started to enjoy challenges. I even looked forward to our daily math multiplication speed tests after lunch. My grade five teacher made them fun, and I pushed myself to improve each day. I didn't realize it then, but those small victories mattered. They were teaching me discipline, focus, and courage, qualities I would later need for a connection far more profound, one that would shape the rest of my life.

When I reflect on those years, I can see that those early struggles, the loneliness, the quiet endurance, and the tiny triumphs were building something inside me. Each challenge was preparing me, even though I had no idea what for.

Shelley Fraser

Chapter Four
The Path to Sister John

In September 1980, I was about to start seventh grade. All the junior high and high school students gathered in the gymnasium to receive their homeroom assignments. I was twelve, maybe thirteen, just returning from Calgary after spending the summer with my mom. I felt nervous about the first day and was relieved when our neighbor, a twelfth-grade student from down the street, asked if I wanted to walk to school with her. Her offer steadied me.

As we approached the school, my nerves rose again. The gym buzzed with older students who were noisy, confident, and familiar with the routine. I spotted a few classmates and slipped in beside them, waiting for our names to be called. I was surprised to see how many Catholic sisters were teaching at the end of the school. I had no idea that one of them would become our homeroom teacher, someone who would change the course of my life.

Her name was Sister John.

She wore the traditional black and white habit, the black veil framing her face. She had glasses, brown eyes, and brown hair. Slender and not very old, she carried herself with quiet authority. She was French, yet her English flowed so smoothly that you could hardly detect an accent. Her voice was even and calm as she called out our names, gathering us together and guiding us toward our classroom. Something about her presence eased my nerves in a way I could not explain.

I still remember walking into her classroom. It faced south, and the large rectangular windows filled the room with warm light. The wooden desks were taller than what I was used to. Blackboards lined the entire right wall and stretched across the front. Her desk sat just beneath a crucifix. I did not know then that she would also be our French teacher.

On that first day, I had not brought any supplies. I went up to her and asked what I would need for the year. She gave me a simple list. That evening, I told my grandfather what I needed, though home life was difficult. His drinking continued to worsen, and I often felt uncertain about how he would react.

As the year began, Sister John asked me one day if I would mind cleaning the blackboards after school. I agreed right away. It was a small task, but to me it meant something. Her request felt like acknowledgment, like she saw me. At that time, neither of my parents were caring for me, and I was often unkempt.

That fall, I sometimes went to the gym to watch sports. Sister John would appear at times on the sidelines, observing. One Monday, she asked me what I thought of the weekend volleyball tournament. I said it was okay. Then she asked if I had noticed one particular girl on the other team. I said yes. It was a simple exchange.

Freshie Day came that fall. Grade seven students were auctioned off to raise money for the school. Despite my chaotic home life, a boy and I ended up being auctioned at the highest price. It felt strange to be valued, even jokingly, but it was one of the few moments in my early adolescence where I felt seen.

Around that time, Sister Cathy taught Social Studies. One day she told me that if I ever had any problems, I could come and talk to her. I said okay and tucked her words away. I did not know then how soon I would need them.

One evening in November, I returned to my grandfather's house and found the door locked. My suitcase was sitting near the garbage can. He had been drinking again. Confused and hurt, I realized I had nowhere to go. I walked to my dad's place, but he was not home, and with his girlfriend there it did not feel safe. Desperate, I turned to an elderly Indigenous woman who lived behind my father's house. She had spoken kindly to me before. When I told her what had happened, she opened her door without hesitation and offered me a place to sleep.

The Morning I Walked Her Home

Her compassion gave me a small sense of safety in a night that felt unbearable.

The next day at school, I told Sister Cathy what had happened. She listened carefully and then said with firm kindness that I could not go back there. She told me I would come with her to the convent until they could figure something out. I was scared. I had only been inside the convent once, back in grade two. She assured me she would speak to Sister Chelsea, the superior at the time.

That night, I had supper with the sisters. Sister John was there too. After the meal, Sister Cathy told me I would stay there for the night. The sisters made me a bed in the basement. For the first time in a long while, I felt like I belonged.

The next evening, after Mass, Sister John walked with me to collect some of my belongings. As we were about to pass the local bar, people were drinking outside near a vehicle. I crossed the street, uneasy, but Sister John stayed on the same side. A man hurled a beer bottle in her direction. She turned quickly and took another route. A moment later, I saw her shadow move across the laundromat window, and I felt a wave of relief. Together we stopped at my dad's and my grandfather's, gathered what I needed, and returned safely to the convent.

Living with the sisters became a source of comfort I had not known before. Evenings were warm and predictable, with snacks, quiet conversations, and sometimes watching television. Sister John often came to check on me, wishing me goodnight with a tenderness I was not used to. Once she gently touched my face and said, "Belle face." For the first time in years, I felt truly safe.

At school, sometimes I would misbehave in Sister John's class just to catch her attention. She was patient with me. She gave me notebooks when I had no paper, writing my name carefully at the top, Shelley, not Shelly. Her small gestures were like anchors, proof that I mattered to someone.

Evenings in the convent were peaceful. In the community room, the sisters crocheted, played cards, or talked softly. Sister John sat with me, teaching me how to pronounce the days of the week in French. She told me I had very good pronunciation. Her encouragement felt like sunlight in a place that had long been dim.

But one evening, I made a mistake. I do not remember what I said, but I blurted out, "You have a big mouth." Her reaction was immediate. She left the room and returned visibly upset. Sister Sandy tried to defend me, saying I had not meant any harm, but Sister John replied, "No, Sandy…" The disappointment in her voice stung deeply. I left the convent briefly, ashamed. When I returned, I saw her walking with another sister. They did not notice me. It took time before our silence eased. Then one day, after class, she gently grabbed my arm and said, "You are hardheaded." I smiled. The tension broke. I sensed in that moment that she was not going to let me fade away.

On December 8, 1980, we celebrated Sister John's birthday. She winked at me as she sat with her cake. That same night, the world learned that John Lennon had been assassinated. The shock rippled through everyone. Yet Christmas was near, and I was preparing to visit my mother in Calgary. Sister John helped me make homemade candles and gave me doilies to bring as gifts. It was thoughtful and personal, something I had rarely experienced. Later that month, a few sisters took me to Prince Albert to buy clothing. When I returned from Calgary, one of them met me at the bus depot and drove me back. I returned with a gingerbread house for them to enjoy.

In January 1981, I learned I would be leaving the convent to stay with another family. I was disappointed. I had found stability and love with the sisters, but I was too young to live there permanently. Shortly after moving, I caught the mumps. When I returned to school, Sister John noticed immediately that I was not well and phoned the family to come get me.

February arrived, and I gave Sister John two Valentine cards. Later I saw her in the hallway reading them, and it warmed me. But life in my new home was difficult. I began drinking. The family complained they were not receiving enough money to care for me. I felt guilty, though it was never my fault. I missed the love, the routine, the tenderness of the convent. Eventually, I was told I would be returning to my mother.

I told Sister John I was leaving. She asked if I would be coming back. I said I didn't know. On my last day, she gave me an envelope with a photo of Jesus and a necklace of the Virgin Mary cradling Him. I left with a social worker and was taken to a youth shelter in Prince Albert until my mother agreed to have me back, on the condition that I go to school. While at the shelter, I often looked at the photo, and the necklace Sister John had given me.

Returning to Calgary mid-year was overwhelming. I struggled to adjust, slipped back into drinking, and missed school. I would call Sister John occasionally. She always asked how school was going. I never said it directly, but I think she knew I was fighting to keep my head above water.

The school year ended, and in September 1981, I made a quiet promise to myself to start fresh. I began praying daily, asking for help. Sister John was still teaching in the small community I had left behind. That fall, I received a letter from her. She included a note from my brother Stewart and joked that he was as slow as molasses in January. Her letters always lifted me. She ended each one with, "Be good. Don't forget your old teacher."

In December 1981, I returned to visit my grandfather. He was genuinely happy to see me and gave me a kiss and a hug. The sisters had called me and invited my brother and me for lunch. I brought them gifts, and they gave me some in return. Sister John asked about my classes. One afternoon, I was at the local store flipping through magazines when she walked in. She placed her hands on my shoulders and said, "I like your hair." My wavy hair was healthy then, and I smiled and said thank you. Then she continued with her errands.

What I admired most about Sister John was her steady, patient, and deeply caring nature. She never judged me, and she rarely scolded me. With her, I felt seen and cared for. And that, more than anything, was what drew me toward her.

Shelley Fraser

Chapter Five
A Weekend of Light

In 1982, I often visited Prince Albert during holidays and stayed with my aunt and uncle. Those trips offered a break from the noise of everyday life, a chance to reconnect with people who made me feel safe. I tried to see Sister John when she visited the "Big House" in Prince Albert, but she was often on retreat. I would leave my number, and she always called back. Each time, the sound of her voice lifted me. There were also times when I visited her in the community of Hope, such as after my grandfather passed away. During those visits, we talked about school and many other things, reconnecting in a way that felt steady and familiar.

The school year of 1982 to 1983 was my final year at St. Joseph's Junior High in Calgary. Years later, in 1993, I learned that Sister John had once taught at another St. Joseph's, an elementary school in Saskatchewan. That small coincidence felt like another quiet thread weaving our lives together.

At St. Joseph's, I enjoyed learning and made good friends. I especially loved playing table tennis, and at lunchtime we gathered around the pool table. But that year also marked the beginning of my drinking with peers. Sometimes we even arrived at school intoxicated. Strangely, there were no suspensions or consequences. It was a confusing mix of freedom and recklessness. I was searching for something, perhaps escape or acceptance, without knowing how to ask for help.

Through it all, I stayed connected with Sister John. I phoned occasionally and wrote letters, and she would reply, even while studying at university that summer. Her words were a steady light, gentle proof that someone cared.

When the 1983 school year ended and high school loomed, I visited Sister John and Sister Cathy at the "Big House."

During one conversation, she said, "I am quite a bit older than you." I did not think much about age then. She was now superior of the convent in a small town near her hometown of Jackson Lake. Before I left, she smiled and said, "You will have to come visit us." The invitation thrilled me.

I made the trip that December. Sister John was teaching junior high and high school a few miles from the convent. I arrived by bus to a town in blackout. The tiny store glowed only with candlelight. I waited there until she arrived with a flashlight. Her appearance in the darkness felt like a quiet rescue, reminding me of another night back in 1980 when she helped me retrieve clothing from my grandfather's house.

In her full habit, she walked with me back to the convent, where the sisters were moving cautiously through the candlelit halls. We had lunch in the kitchen, and I met sisters I had not known before, including Sister Doris, whom I would later reconnect with in 2007 at the Bounty Reserve, and Sister Yvonne, a petite woman I would also meet again years later.

The weekend was unforgettable. Sister John brought me to meet her aunt and uncle in town. I met the priest's housekeeper, a large, spirited woman whose humor filled the room. I helped paint the convent with Sister John's cousin and another relative. I went cross-country skiing, played cards with the sisters and local seniors, and even played pool with Sister John.

One afternoon, I overheard her say to another sister, "That is my number one student." The words warmed me deeply. One evening, she came downstairs while I was watching television, and we talked until 12:45 AM, even though she had to work the next day. That conversation still feels vivid, her presence steady and her attention genuine.

When it was time to leave, several of the sisters kissed me on the cheek, including Sister John. I returned to Calgary with a full heart. A week later, a Christmas card arrived signed by the sisters. Inside was a note from Sister John that read, "You are great. Love, Sister John," along with a request that said, "Have your counsellor call me." She included both her work and home numbers. In return, I sent her a card and a few small gifts, grateful for the kindness she showed me.

That weekend remains a treasure. It taught me that love does not always announce itself. Sometimes it arrives in candlelight, in shared laughter, or in a handwritten note. The convent no longer houses sisters and now operates as a hotel, but every time I visit, memories return. It is Sister John who made that place unforgettable.

Shelley Fraser

Chapter Six
Growth, Grace, and a Weekend in May

The 1983-1984 was a whirlwind year, full of activity, responsibility, and unexpected lessons. I was beginning to feel the weight and wonder of growing up, caught between duty and the desire to be seen. I threw myself into high school life and proudly served as vice president of the student council. My days were filled with leadership duties, friendships, and a growing sense of independence. After lunch, I was often found on the PA system making announcements. Years later, some students still remembered my voice echoing through the halls.

In May, I made another weekend trip to visit Sister John. I was excited to see her, but the journey did not go as planned. Somewhere along the way, my luggage was lost on the bus. I felt frustrated and helpless, but I refused to let it ruin the visit. I washed the clothes I had and made do. It became a quiet lesson in resilience. Thankfully, the luggage was found just before I returned to Calgary.

During that visit, I told Sister John I was running for school president. She smiled and said, "Be sure to let us know if you win." Her encouragement meant more than she realized. The sisters had planned a picnic that weekend, and Sister John also invited me to join her and her aunt and uncle for a fishing trip. Instead, I chose to go with the priest's housekeeper, who took me on a drive to a nearby creek. I enjoyed her company immensely; she had a way of making me laugh and feel at ease.

I helped around the convent as well, mowing the lawn and tending the garden. One morning, after staying out late the night before, I overslept and missed breakfast. Sister John sat at the kitchen table with her arms crossed. I smiled at her while I ate, but I could feel her disappointment. She did not need to say a word. Her silence said enough. I knew I had let her down, even just a little. The next day, before returning to Calgary, I visited the priest's housekeeper again and ended up spending the night there. Sister John never found out.

Back in Calgary, the school year unfolded with unexpected success. I received four awards that year, including Student of the Month. Those moments felt like sunlight breaking through, affirmation that things were finally coming together. And to top it off, I won the school presidency by acclamation. No one ran against me, whether it was confidence in me or simply lack of interest. My homeroom and typing teacher even helped design posters for my campaign.

That year was a turning point. It was a year of growth, of learning to navigate responsibility, and of continuing to cherish my connection with Sister John, even when things did not go perfectly. She had a way of grounding me, reminding me that grace is not about perfection, but presence.

The Morning I Walked Her Home

Shelley Fraser

Chapter Seven
The Weight Behind the Crown

In June 1984, I was elected school president at a high school of more than 500 students. It was an incredible feeling to be entrusted with leadership. For the first time, I felt like my voice truly mattered. People listened, and I realized I was no longer just surviving; I was leading.

The school year of 1984-1985 quickly became one of the busiest and most rewarding chapters of my life. I also worked in the school administration office during lunchtime, earning a small salary. I felt proud to contribute in a meaningful way and to be part of the work that kept the school running.

Our school organized food hamper drives and UNICEF fundraisers, with each classroom competing to raise the most donations. I was determined that our homeroom would come out on top, and we did. We were recognized with both the Food Hamper and UNICEF awards, a moment of pride that felt larger than ourselves.

Later, I was contacted by another student council president from a Calgary high school, inviting us to join a citywide UNICEF challenge. I accepted, unsure of what our school could contribute. Yet we ended up surpassing every other high school in Calgary and winning the UNICEF challenge. Looking back, the victory was not just about pennies collected. It was about discovering what a community can accomplish when everyone feels part of something larger.

That year also brought many personal milestones. I received another Student of the Month award, along with the Citizenship and Psychology Awards. I earned a trip for two to the Solid Gold Dance-a-thon and raised the most money for Alberta's Children's Hospital, going door to door in the community. Our school principal invited me to join him for lunch at the school's Christmas dinner, and I was later selected for a two-day paid trip to Lethbridge, Alberta. I also competed in the Alberta Provincial Typing Competition.

The Morning I Walked Her Home

Beyond academics, I was active on the yearbook committee, helped paint the girls' washroom, participated in school dances, and remained on the school honor roll. Before graduation, I was asked whether I wanted to be class historian or valedictorian. I chose class historian. It was an unforgettable year, filled with pride, purpose, and connection.

Yet beneath all that success, a shadow had begun to form. I started drinking alcohol, even attending class under the influence. I did not fully understand why. Perhaps it was unresolved pain, or something deeper I had not yet faced. I smiled through assemblies, gave speeches, and kept showing up, but inside, I was unraveling. I knew only that I was hurting, and I did not know how to name it.

During that time, I called Sister John a few times. She sent me a graduation card, a simple but profound gesture that reminded me I was not alone. Her handwriting felt like a steady hand on my shoulder, anchoring me in a time when I felt unmoored.

But when graduation came, the excitement and momentum of the year vanished almost overnight. The joy, the sense of belonging, the recognition, it all seemed to disappear. That school had given me so much, and I had poured my heart into it. Years later, I still remember my high school English teacher saying, "You were one of the best school presidents we ever had."

It is important to recognize that high-achieving young people often carry invisible burdens. Unspoken traumas quietly shape the present. I was learning that success does not erase pain. It only masks it for a while.

The school year of 1984-1985 was a year of triumph, but also a year of reckoning. And although I did not know it then, the real work of healing and becoming was only just beginning.

Shelley Fraser

Shelley's high school graduation photo.

School Clubs

Shelley with the Art Club, 1984–1985.

Shelley with the Bridge Builders Club, 1984–1985.

School Activities

Shelley with the school UNICEF graph.

UNICEF

In October 1984, classrooms collected $425 in pennies, nickels, and dimes for UNICEF, with Room 315 contributing $109. As student council president, Shelley was part of the school's effort that won the city-wide competition, beating all other Calgary high schools in raising the most money to support children in underdeveloped countries.

Shelley in the center with classmates, Halloween 1984.

School Activities (continued)

Shelley with the Yearbook Committee, 1984–1985.

Shelley as student council president with her student council,
1984–1985.

School Activities (continued)

Shelley was one of the recipients of Student of the Month
honors, 1984–1985.

The Morning I Walked Her Home

Chapter Eight
1986

After graduating from high school, I started working at a printing press in Calgary. I was stepping into adulthood, but I still carried the weight of everything I had not yet faced. During that time, Sister John returned to my former hometown of Hope, where we had first met in 1980. She continued teaching junior and senior high students, quietly building a legacy of care, steadiness, and devotion.

In April 1986, I visited my aunt and uncle in Prince Albert and decided to see my dad, my brothers, and Sister John. Nearly two years had passed since we last met. She welcomed me with her familiar warmth, and we sat together in the kitchen while she mended a piece of clothing. At one point, she went to her room and returned with a photo of the class I would have graduated with if I had remained in that community. In that simple gesture, I felt something I had not realized I had been longing for. I felt remembered not for what I achieved but for who I was. It was a quiet, touching moment that spoke volumes about her thoughtfulness.

A few months later, my aunt and uncle celebrated their twenty fifth wedding anniversary. I brought my school awards and a large graduation photo to show Sister John what I had accomplished since leaving. She was proud. She even asked if she could bring them to school and show the staff. I gladly agreed.

The next day, my younger brother came to me with a grin. He said, "Sister John put your awards on the ledge of the blackboard. The students were looking at them." Then he added, trying to hide a smile, "I felt dumb because my sister was smarter than me." Even though I wasn't there, I felt seen. It was as if my story had found its way back. Sister John had hoped I would visit the school that day, but I didn't go. Something inside me felt out of place, as though that chapter had already closed. When she later asked, "Why didn't you come?" I had no real answer, only the sense that I was already becoming someone new.

Still, I told the sisters, "Sister John was a big part of all this." And she truly was. I would not have achieved what I did without her guidance and care. She entered my life at a moment when I urgently needed someone who could see potential where I could not.

Around that time, Sister John and my mother met for the first time. Their meeting was brief and slightly awkward. My mom waited in the car while I went inside to tell Sister John she was outside. Sister John said she would like to meet her. She walked out, offered her hand, and they exchanged a few polite words. Then my mom and I drove off.

During those years, my friends and I behaved like any other young teenagers. We cruised up and down Main Street with the music turned up as loud as the speakers would allow. Songs like Bruce Springsteen's "Glory Days," Elvis Presley's "Jailhouse Rock," Dire Straits' "Walk of Life," Heart's "If Looks Could Kill," and Marty Robbins' "The Story of My Life" created the soundtrack of our youth.

We often spotted Sister John standing on the sidewalk in front of the convent. Her arms were folded as she watched us drift by. Her presence felt steady and constant, like a lighthouse that guided and observed without judging too harshly. We would smile, pretending not to notice her subtle hint of disapproval, and eventually our laughter would fade, and I would pull the car over and talk with her. With a quiet grin she would say, "I don't mind modern music, but we have some older sisters in the house."

A few days later, as I prepared to return to Calgary, I visited Sister John one last time. I told her my mother no longer wanted me to see her. The news visibly upset her. She said quietly, "I am deceived." I asked if she had ever had to end a friendship before. She answered, "Yes, and I think of her when it is sunny outside." The room was dim, and the sadness in her eyes felt heavy. I left that night deeply unsettled and unable to sleep.

The next day, I drove back into the small community. A friend and I were circling the streets with music flowing through the car when we passed the convent. My friend said, "There is Sister John." She rushed outside, and another sister reached out as if to hold her back. She approached my car window and asked how I slept. I told her I had slept well, hiding the truth that I had not slept at all. I was hurting too.

She asked if I was returning to Prince Albert. When I said yes, she replied without hesitation, "I will go with you. Let me pack." And she did. During the drive, she spoke about my mother. She said, "Your mom cannot tell you who you can see." I agreed, though I was nineteen and still learning how to stand on my own and define myself without fear.

Later that July, I volunteered at the Special Olympics in Calgary. The experience gave me a sense of purpose and joy. I worked alongside Calgary Flames hockey players such as Lanny McDonald and Tim Hunter, and for the first time in a long while, I felt part of something larger than myself.

Then in August, tragedy struck. My mother received a call. There had been a death at my father's farm. My stepmother had taken her own life while my father was outside. One of her children had to climb through a window to unlock the door and found his mother on the floor. My father was in shock, pacing the house and unable to understand how and why everything had changed so suddenly.

The next day, I called Sister John and told her what had happened. She was spending the summer in Prince Albert at the "Big House," and without hesitation she said, "Come get me. I will go to the funeral with you." A few days later, I picked her up along with my brothers, and together we traveled to the Bounty Reserve for the funeral. As we walked into the church, Sister John held tightly to my arm. Her grip conveyed everything, including grief shared, pain acknowledged, and love offered without expectation.

After the service, I drove her back to Prince Albert. That evening, I told her once more that I thought we should end our friendship. She stared out the window and would not look at me. When my brother arrived to pick me up, she finally spoke. She said, "I am not ending my six or seven-year friendship with you." I left feeling confused, unsure why I kept trying to distance myself. I had not yet learned how to accept love that did not demand anything in return.

Despite my inner turmoil, our friendship continued. In October, I returned for Thanksgiving with my mother, who stayed behind to visit my father. That same weekend, Sister John invited my stepsiblings and me for lunch. She had been teaching some of them at school. We spoke often on the phone, our connection persisting even when I tried to pull away.

In December, I returned for Christmas and spent it with my father. Sister John was in Prince Albert, and one of the sisters said she would return with me. We shared a meaningful conversation during the drive. That week, she baked a beautiful cake for me to take to the farm and share with the kids. It must have taken her hours to prepare. I gave her Christmas gifts, and one of the sisters took a photo of us together.

But soon I began drinking again. Sister John, patient as always, would offer me coffee to help steady myself. One evening, she invited me to attend midnight Mass with her and asked me to gather the kids from the farm. I went, although some of us had been drinking. I did not sit with her, and I am not even sure she knew we were there.

Once again, I began to push her away. I was angry and overwhelmed by a deep sense of inadequacy, and I didn't yet understand the roots of those feelings. When I reflect now, I see that being close to Sister John triggered everything I had tried so hard to bury, including pain, confusion, and unresolved trauma. She represented love and safety, a place where I was seen without judgment. That frightened me, because it brought long-hidden wounds to the surface, ones I wasn't accustomed to facing. Yet somewhere inside, I knew that confronting those wounds was the only way forward.

Shelley Fraser

Chapter Nine
The Turning Point

1987 began with a sense of hope. My connection with Sister John felt steady, and one afternoon my stepsister told me that Sister John had displayed photos of me in her classroom. I felt surprised and deeply touched. In that small gesture, I sensed that she saw me not for my accomplishments, but for my journey. It was a quiet affirmation of the place I held in her life. Yet I was slowly learning that hope does not erase the echoes of old pain.

Beneath the surface, I was still struggling. My drinking continued, and the weight I carried remained unspoken and unresolved. Although Sister John and I talked often over the phone, the tone of our conversations began to change. We disagreed more frequently, and at times she would say, "I love it when you get mad." Her words left me confused. I did not understand why she said it or what she meant. All I knew was that something once sacred felt suddenly fragile, and I had no language for the emotions rising inside me.

During that time, I also became friends with the local Catholic priest, a monsignor who had presided over my father's girlfriend's funeral. He was kind, and our friendship lasted until his passing. Sister John would visit with him from time to time as well.

By late spring, I began to sense the strain in my relationship with Sister John. Some of her comments unsettled me, especially coming from someone in her position. The dynamic between us was becoming emotionally complicated, and I could feel the relationship shifting into something deeper than I knew how to handle. I was still young and lacked the insight to fully understand what was happening, but I knew something had changed. In hindsight, I believe Sister John may have begun to feel conflicted, caught between her role as a religious sister and the closeness we had developed.

In June, I learned that Sister John would be moving to another province, and the news filled me with mixed emotions. I knew the distance would change things. On the day she was to leave for Prince Albert for the summer, I drove her and Sister Anne to the "Big House." I didn't know then that she would become the superior at her new residence. Before she left, she told me I could visit her there.

Throughout July and August, we spent time together. We went for walks, stopped for ice cream at Dairy Queen, and she would call me. She even came to see me when I started a new job at one of the local stores. Her presence remained comforting, a steady light during a time when everything inside me felt uncertain and shifting.

That same year, I enrolled in a Catholic Bible college in Alberta, hoping it would bring clarity to my life. I was searching for peace, yet the storm inside me had not settled. My drinking continued, and the emotional weight I carried made it difficult to focus. It did not take long for me to realize that the Bible college was not the right place for me. Even during my time there, Sister John would call to check on me and speak with the director.

In November, I was admitted to a detox center and later attended a treatment facility in Saskatchewan. It was the hardest decision I had ever made and the bravest. I committed to sobriety and remained sober for many years. While in treatment, I called Sister John occasionally, but over time our phone conversations dwindled and stopped altogether in early 1988.

For some time afterward, I continued to write her letters. Eventually, I made the difficult choice to end our communication. Letting go felt like losing a part of myself, but I understood that healing required distance. Did I miss her? Without question. But I also knew it was time to build my own life, one that was not defined by the past or shaped by the pain I was trying to overcome.

It would be some years before I saw Sister John again. But she had walked with me through the darkest valleys, and her light stayed with me, even in silence. The bond we shared, and the impact she had on my life, never faded.

The Morning I Walked Her Home

42

Chapter Ten
When Silence Speaks

In the fall of 1990, Sister John returned to the small community where I had first met her as a seventh grader in 1980. I was surprised to hear she was back and still teaching junior and senior high school. Three years had passed since we last saw each other, yet this time something felt unfamiliar. The relationship carried a strain I had not expected. I had imagined our reunion many times, but nothing prepared me for the silence that greeted me instead.

I wrote to Sister John, letting her know I would be visiting my father and hoped to see her. When I arrived, my friends and I spent time driving through the town, music blaring, laughter filling the car, and old memories returning. But the joy of those earlier years with Sister John was missing. The energy felt distant and disconnected.

One afternoon, we saw Sister John walking down the street with the superior. I did not stop or call out. Later that weekend, I asked my stepbrother to deliver a note to the convent. When he knocked, the superior opened the door and said, "If you don't tell me what's in this note, I am going to drop it on the floor." Then Sister John stepped forward and said, "I would prefer not to see Shelley, and I am sure she will understand why."

When my stepbrother told me, I was stunned. Her words felt like a door closing, and I was left standing on the other side, confused and hurt. How was I supposed to understand something that had never been explained? I was not a mind reader, and I had no idea what she meant. Understanding would come only years later.

That same weekend, we drove past the convent one evening and saw a silhouette seated at the kitchen table with the lights turned off, a quiet and unsettling sight. It was Sister John, watching us through the window. She remained there for at least ten minutes. For someone who claimed she did not want contact, she was still observing from a distance. It left me confused. I sensed she was wrestling with her own emotions, torn between personal connection and the boundaries she was expected to maintain. I believe she felt she had crossed an invisible line, not in any inappropriate way, but through genuine care, and now felt obligated to retreat.

It was around this time that boundaries became the norm between us. I must admit I didn't like it, but I had to respect her position if I wanted any hope of reconciliation.

A few days later, I returned to Calgary and called her. I said, "Since you don't want this friendship anymore, I would like the return of my belongings." She answered, "No, I don't want it and all I have is your graduation photo." I asked her to return it. She eventually sent it back through my stepbrother, and shortly afterward she did not show up at school.

Did I genuinely want the photo back? Absolutely not. It was never about the photo. What I longed for was the connection, the acknowledgment, and the warmth that once accompanied it. I found it telling that she had brought my graduation photo with her when she returned to the community. Sisters usually pack lightly, and the fact that she chose to bring it stayed with me. I was hurt and emotionally exhausted from trying to reach out and getting nowhere. Sister John could be stubborn, and I was beginning to feel defeated.

One day, a friend of mine called the convent and spoke with the superior, asking whether there was any way to mend things between us. The superior answered, "Sister John got too close, and now she does not know what to do, and I cannot tell her what to do." In that moment, it occurred to me that perhaps we had both stepped into a space neither of us knew how to navigate.

With time, I have come to realize how difficult this situation must have been for Sister John. She may have been advised to distance herself. She may have believed it was the safest choice. I never honestly believed she wanted to end our connection. Catholic sisters take vows of celibacy, obedience, and poverty. If her superior instructed her to avoid personal attachments, she would have been obligated to follow her vow of obedience.

For me, the rejection was what cut the deepest. I had formed a connection with Sister John at an early age, and her silence felt like abandonment. There had been so many moments filled with joy, closeness, and genuine excitement. To be honest, the experience with Sister John and the other sisters shook my faith. I wrestled with the values they were meant to embody. It did not feel godly. It felt cold.

With time, I came to understand that the Catholic Church, as an institution, often suppresses emotional expression through its vows, boundaries, and the expectation of unspoken love. You do not need to be religious to recognize its imperfections.

Even so, I held on to the belief that something deeper had been at work. Something more meaningful than either of us could fully name. I carried that truth with me, quiet and unresolved, yet still sacred.

The Morning I Walked Her Home

Shelley Fraser

Chapter Eleven
Roots of the Pain

In 1993, I was still trying to understand the pain that lived inside me. I could not connect the dots between my emotions and their origins. One day, a friend suggested I attend a treatment program in the United States, something that might help me uncover the forces that had shaped me for so many years. After learning more about the program, I decided to go.

It is important to acknowledge that the pain did not begin with Sister John. It existed long before anything between us started to unravel. I believe it began when I left the small community in 1981, although at the time I did not understand why I felt the way I did. As a young teenager, I turned to drinking to numb something I could not yet name.

I grew up in a fractured home. My parents divorced when I was young, and for a time I lived with a grandfather who struggled with alcoholism. I was also a victim of abuse by neighbors. I never knew either of my grandmothers. My mother lost her mother at age ten and was raised in foster homes. My father lost his mother at age four and grew up with a father who battled alcoholism and unresolved grief. There was a generational pattern of maternal absence that felt almost impossible to break.

My parents married young and had four children. I was the eldest, followed by two younger brothers and a baby sister who tragically died in a car accident at eleven months old in May 1972. I remember that day with striking clarity. It was sunny when my mother took us to visit her brother in Prince Albert. The car was overcrowded with at least twelve people, no seat belts, and a driver without a license.

I can still picture my baby sister on my mother's lap, sharing a bag of Cheezies, sipping orange pop, and wearing a little white bonnet. None of us were secure. Then came the tire blowout. I regained consciousness lying in shattered glass, my back aching as I tried to understand what had happened. The car had flipped. A doctor from the

The Morning I Walked Her Home

Shellbrook hospital arrived. I saw a large potato sack on the grass and was told not to look back. At the time, I did not know she had died.

My grandfather gave up his burial plot in another cemetery so she could be laid to rest. The owner of the vehicle had no insurance, and my parents could not afford the funeral. My father was devastated, and my mother lived with guilt. Their grief seeped into the fabric of their marriage. I often stayed with my grandfather to escape the tension. I was growing more independent, yet I was also distancing myself from the chaos around me.

I also witnessed troubling things. I remember my father throwing my mother's clothing into the bush and searching for her while I was with her. When I was eight or nine, I would help my mother with laundry down the street. That was when the abuse began, first from an elderly man and later from another neighbor. I did not understand what was happening, and I never told anyone. Years later, I learned I had not been the only victim. What disturbed me most was how many people knew these men were predators, yet no one stepped in. Society often protects the perpetrator and leaves victims to carry emotional scars for life.

The roots of my pain were intergenerational. I was carrying the weight of my parents' and grandfather's losses, abandonment, trauma, and grief. The absence of maternal figures, the instability of home, and the tragedy of my sister's death created a foundation of confusion that no child should have had to face. Early childhood trauma, when left unaddressed, shapes a life in ways no one can anticipate.

As I revisit the years between 1986 and 1992, I now see that they were some of the most painful. Sister John was living in the same community where I had been abused and where so many family memories held darkness. Being there triggered flashbacks I did not recognize at the time. I pushed her away, not because she had harmed me, but because I feared being hurt again. Sister John cared deeply, but I could not distinguish love from danger.

Eventually, I began researching trauma and behavior, and I started to understand how my past had shaped the choices I made, such as avoiding school at age ten, moving to a large city, drinking, and distancing myself from Sister John. These feelings had been buried for years.

In 1993, I finally saw a light at the end of the tunnel. For the first time, I felt I was not only surviving but reclaiming my story. I reviewed old school records and other documents and decided to press charges against one of my abusers. That decision became an act of reclaiming my power and a declaration of strength.

I began writing to Sister John, sharing what I was learning about myself. By then, she was teaching elementary school in another part of Saskatchewan.

That summer, she was on retreat in Prince Albert. I left flowers for her, and she placed them in the chapel at the "Big House." I also left a note at the front desk with my contact number. Then something unexpected happened. As we drove past in the vehicle, I saw her walking along the sidewalk, as if she were looking for me. She paused and glanced in our direction. I did not stop. I was afraid she might be upset, and it felt like a moment I was not yet ready to face.

Later, when my friend James met her, she asked, "You guys didn't go back to that small community, did you?" Her voice carried concern. She called me afterward, but I did not return her call.

Finally, in August, I gathered the courage to reach out and asked if we could meet. She agreed. Nearly six years had passed since we had last seen each other face to face, and I was nervous.

When we met, she asked, "Why didn't you call back?" I answered, "I don't know." We began to talk. During our conversation, she sat in a chair working on something for school. Then she made a comment that caught me off guard. She said, "I'm feeling there is more." I didn't know what she meant. I struggled to read between the lines with her. It felt as if she was reaching for something deeper, and I wasn't sure how to meet her there.

The Morning I Walked Her Home

As I began to process the abuse I experienced as a young girl, the path toward healing led me to question how Sister John felt toward me. Her words stayed with me, although I could not fully grasp their meaning. I sensed she was speaking about her own emotions, which added another layer of uncertainty to an already confusing time. I opened my life to people I trusted, yet many expected more from me.

As I prepared to leave, she broke a flower from a nearby plant and handed it to me. It was a quiet gesture filled with meaning. It was not just a flower. It was her way of saying she still cared. That moment marked the beginning of a new chapter, one in which healing had finally begun.

Shelley Fraser

51

Chapter Twelve
Uniforms and Unspoken Bonds

In June of 1995, I had not seen Sister John in quite some time, nor had I written to her for a while. When I learned she was retiring from teaching young people, I felt compelled to reach out. Something in me still needed her presence, even if I did not yet know how to say it. I called and asked if we could meet. When we did, I brought her a cake, a card, and a small gift.

There was a noticeable change in her appearance. She no longer wore the uniform I had always associated with her, and it took me by surprise. I was shocked, and truthfully, I never fully adjusted to seeing her in plain clothing. To me, the uniform held meaning. It symbolized something sacred, something stable. Without it, she felt like a different person, as if a thread between us had frayed. That was the first time I realized how deeply clothing can reveal or protect one's identity. Though I tried to accept the change, I must admit it took time to get used to.

During that visit, Sister John told me she was leaving for Ottawa to study and gave me her address so I could write to her. That summer, I was working with the Royal Canadian Mounted Police and studying at university. I went to see her again, this time wearing my own uniform. She came downstairs and seemed surprised to see me dressed that way. For a moment, I wondered if she recognized how far I had come.

Before her departure, some of her relatives and I organized a barbecue in her honor. When I reached out, she said, "I know what's going on." I picked her up at the "Big House" in Prince Albert. She was waiting outside with the superior who had once remarked, "She got too close and didn't know what to do." It struck me to see the two of them together as I pulled up.

We made the two-hour journey, and during the drive I showed her a photo album of my family. She paused over one picture and asked,

"Who is this?" I told her, "That's my mother's younger sister, my aunt Jenny." As we neared our destination, Sister John asked to be dropped off at her brother's house, perhaps to rest before the gathering.

She arrived later with her brother, and I was introduced to him and her sister. The barbecue itself was pleasant, but I felt a strange awkwardness, not because of the people, but because of Sister John's presence. I think I was nervous. We had not shared much in recent years, and the emotional distance between us felt heavy. I wanted it to feel like old times, but something had shifted, and I did not know how to bridge it.

After the event, Sister John and I drove back to Prince Albert. It was close to midnight when we arrived. We did not speak much during the ride. I dropped her off, and we shook hands. A few days later, we had a minor disagreement.

It was not until later that I noticed the similarities between Sister John and my Aunt Jenny. They both wore glasses, had slender builds, brown eyes, and hair, and shared a gift for communicating with others. Years later, I told Sister John that she had reminded me of my aunt.

When I was young, Aunt Jenny made things for me, gave me gifts, and told me I was her favorite niece. Long before I met Sister John, she was the one I wrote letters to. So, when I began writing to Sister John, the skill and the impulse were already there. Aunt Jenny took me on trips and sent me things in the mail, teaching me the meaning of thoughtful gestures.

Shortly after Sister John left, I sent her a basket of fruit when she arrived in Ottawa. Even in her absence, I still wanted to reach out, to offer something thoughtful, something that simply said, I am still thinking of you. Because even when words fail, gestures still carry the weight of love.

The Morning I Walked Her Home

Shelley working with the R.C.M.P.

Shelley Fraser

Chapter Thirteen
Echoes of Broken Trust

In 1995-1996, I finally decided to write about my past, my trauma, how I survived it, and my family and school years. The book was called *Broken Trust*. Writing it was both healing and painful. Each page felt like peeling back a wound I had learned to hide. I had to revisit memories I had long buried, including the time I tried to press charges against one of my abusers, only to learn the court would not prosecute because of his age.

The story quickly drew public attention. Newspapers in both Alberta and Saskatchewan ran articles about it, and I was interviewed on television and radio in Calgary. It felt surreal, my pain, once private, now echoed through airwaves and headlines. Still, I wrote as honestly as I could. My life had never been easy, but I had a story to share, and I wanted other survivors to know they were not alone.

My friend Bonnie, who was studying to become a social worker, helped edit the manuscript. Her boyfriend, Julian, an English teacher, designed the cover. Bonnie believed deeply in the book. "We need to make the story just right," she said, "so that others can understand and feel seen in their own experiences as victims." Together, we worked hard to make it meaningful.

Once published, *Broken Trust* was stocked at Coles Bookstore in Prince Albert and sold out quickly. Coles called asking for more copies. Many of the buyers were from the small French community where I grew up. Curiosity ran high; people wanted to know who was in the story.

I mailed a copy to Sister John, who was still on sabbatical in Ottawa. After reading it, she admitted she had not known half of what I had endured. "The past wasn't healthy," she said. When I called her a week later, she asked how many copies had been printed, her curiosity quiet but present.

In the spring of 1996, I visited a friend near Ottawa and arranged to see Sister John. She suggested I stay at the YWCA; it was affordable and close to her place. She came by once, but I was not there. Eventually, we met. Her first question was, "How is your room?" I replied, "It'll do." We visited Parliament, had supper, and went to the IMAX theater. I was fine until the theater, when a wave of anger I could not explain rose up. She noticed but did not ask.

The next morning, she called and said there was a change of plans and invited me for breakfast at her apartment. She made eggs and toast and told me she had bought a pair of slacks with the gift certificate I had given her. As I was leaving, she said softly, "You're very deep to me." I was not sure what she meant, but her words stayed with me, gentle and lingering, like a melody I could not interpret, beautiful and unfinished. Afterward, I wondered what kind of relationship we really had. Her words often left me puzzled, uncertain of their meaning.

That evening, I called her after having a few drinks. My emotions were raw. I told her how much the pulling close and then pushing away had affected me. As I spoke, she rubbed her leg continuously, almost nervously.

She asked, "Shelley, have you been drinking?"

"Yes," I answered.

The next day, before returning to Alberta, I called her again and said, "You may hear from me, or you may not." She was silent. That ended our conversation.

That summer, Coles invited me for a book signing, and I accepted. I also attended a barbecue hosted by the Prince Albert Crisis Unit and donated part of my book sales to them. *Broken Trust* was placed in several Saskatchewan libraries.

Later that summer, Sister John returned to Saskatchewan. We had another disagreement. I said sharply, "Don't you ever hurt a young person like you hurt me." She looked at me but said nothing. I think she was stunned by my words. I walked away. Afterward, my friend Darlene, who knew our history well, spoke with her. They sat together outside on the steps. She told Darlene, "Maybe I influenced Shelley the wrong way." I wondered if that was guilt speaking.

I continued with work and school. In December, I saw Sister John at a priest's funeral, but we did not speak. Later, I visited her at home. She thanked me for the bouquet I had sent. We talked briefly, then I left. She kept her distance, and I walked away not knowing what had gone wrong. I was exhausted. The friendship felt impossible to maintain. I would not see her again until the spring of 1998.

Years later, I realized the pain between us came largely from miscommunication. I think Sister John feared expressing her feelings directly. Instead, she spoke in metaphors, leaving me to interpret the spaces between her words. I felt the restraint, the resistance, and the hurt. Eventually, I had to let the relationship go, though I was not sure for how long.

Still, I knew I mattered to her. In 1993, she had said, "I am feeling there is more." And in Ottawa in 1996, she told me, "You're very deep to me." Those words lingered, tender, confusing, meaningful, yet not enough to understand what she really meant.

Shelley Fraser

Chapter Fourteen
Struck but Still Standing

On February 6, 1997, in Calgary, my life nearly ended.

Around 4:45 p.m., I had just finished writing my next short story, *New Beginnings*, a piece about healing. Only hours after reflecting on recovery, I was abruptly thrust into survival. As I walked home from university and stepped toward a crosswalk where I had the right of way, a sudden force struck me. Time seemed to slow and fear tightened in my chest. Before I could grasp what had happened, I was already lying on the pavement. I had been hit by a vehicle. In that moment, the first person who came to mind was Sister John.

Disoriented, I heard voices around me. A man tried to help me up, but I could not move. Someone called an ambulance. When it arrived, paramedics cut away my clothing, checked my pulse, and worked quickly to stabilize me. Blood seeped from the left side of my head. My blood pressure dropped. My body shook uncontrollably, cold, shocked, trembling. I felt exposed and fragile, as though I no longer had control over my own body.

At the hospital, the shaking gradually stopped. I needed stitches. My face and jaw were swollen, my elbow scraped, and I had a severe concussion. The impact had jolted me violently. I had struck the pavement hard, rolled off the hood of the car, and landed with force.

Darlene picked me up from the hospital. For the next few days, I was monitored for mental and physical stability. The next morning, I could barely get out of bed. My head was foggy. My jaw throbbed. My face was tender and swollen.

The driver who hit me was Russian and did not have a license. The irony was cruel. My baby sister had been killed by someone who also had no license. It felt like history trying to repeat itself. But I survived.

Now I had to focus solely on healing. I could not carry anyone else's burdens. I had to start looking after myself. Recovery became my full-time work, with loneliness as its quiet companion. It took months of massage therapy, physical therapy, and surgery to repair my jaw. I did little in 1997 except try to recover.

Reading the doctor's report later, one line stood out to me. It was a miracle that Shelley did not sustain major injuries. Considering the impact, it felt true. That year, many pedestrians were struck and killed. I had been spared. It felt like a sign that my time was not up. My story was not finished, and maybe it was meant to help others find their own strength.

Despite everything, my second book was eventually published. Once again, Coles Bookstore in Prince Albert stocked it, and copies sold.

The Morning I Walked Her Home

Shelley Fraser

Chapter Fifteen
Reconnecting with Sister John

By the spring of 1998, I was feeling much better. After doing some healing, I began to feel like myself again.

I reconnected with Charlene, a friend from school. She lived in Saskatoon, and we had both been in Sister John's class back in 1980. Together, we visited some of the people we used to know, sharing laughs and memories and recalling the nicknames we had given them.

One day I said, "Why don't we go visit Sister John? I am sure she'd be happy to see you." Charlene, her friend, and I planned a trip. I told Charlene, "You and your friend can visit her on your own. She will be delighted."

Charlene spent at least two hours with Sister John. They talked about school, life, and everything in between. At one point, Sister John asked, "Where is Shelley?" Later, Charlene's friend told me, "She asked about you several times." Hearing that touched something deep in me. Despite the silence, I still mattered to her.

The next evening, I visited Sister John myself. When I arrived, she said, "I knew those girls had to have come with you." We chatted for a while, even though it was late. There were no heavy conversations, no unresolved issues, just a quiet understanding that we were all right. Everything felt calm and settled between us.

I didn't know then how deeply that evening would stay with me. It became a gentle reminder that even broken connections can find their way back to stillness.

It would be the last time I saw Sister John at that residence. She moved to the Bounty Reserve in 1999, and I wouldn't see her again until 2001.

That night of reconnection reminded me that even the most fragile ties can endure, and as life moved forward, I would learn that resilience is not only about surviving the past but also about finding strength in what remains.

The Morning I Walked Her Home

Shelley Fraser

Chapter Sixteen
A Journey Through Pain and Service

In 1999, while living in Calgary, I began experiencing serious health issues. It felt as though my body was betraying me just as I was starting to find my footing again. One day, as I headed downstairs to do laundry, a sharp, severe pain shot through my back. The discomfort was constant, and rest became impossible. Eventually, I was diagnosed with a large blood clot in my left thigh, nearly six inches long. It took several trips to the hospital before anything was done. The swelling became so intense that it even blocked my ability to urinate.

I was hospitalized for nearly two weeks and required daily injections for three months. Walking was impossible during that time. It was frightening and exhausting, especially knowing that if the clot had not been treated properly, it could have been fatal. Lying in that hospital bed, I felt powerless but also determined not to let this break me. That year, I could not do much because of the pain in my leg, but whenever I felt well enough, I tried to visit friends and family in Saskatchewan.

Alongside the blood clot, I was grappling with chronic fatigue syndrome from the earlier car accident, battling intense muscle spasms, and had recently developed shingles. Despite all of this, I found strength and joy in volunteering. I offered my time to the Royal Canadian Legion and genuinely enjoyed the experience. It reminded me that even when my body was weak, my spirit could still stand. Before that, I had served as a board director for Local 87 of the Métis Nation of Alberta.

Volunteering has always been in my blood. I remember selling tickets for my mother's upgrading school when I was just eight or nine years old. I would go out into the community without hesitation; I was not shy. Even in school, I was the type who loved helping others and getting involved. Giving my time has always been something I cherished. Service became my way of reclaiming joy, proof that pain did not define me. Purpose did.

The Morning I Walked Her Home

Chapter Seventeen
The Year of the Millennium

The turn of the century felt like a new beginning, a moment that invited reflection. I was still carrying some old wounds, but something about the new millennium made me hopeful, as if healing might finally be possible. Many of us paused to consider where our lives were heading. For me, medical issues remained an ongoing challenge. Healing was slow.

I had not reached out to Sister John in quite some time. Life had carried us in different directions, and although my intuition sensed she had moved elsewhere, I didn't know where she had gone. One day, I called the "Big House" in Prince Albert to ask where she was living. They told me she had moved to the Bounty Reserve to do Native ministry work, something she had been devoted to for a few years. The Bounty Reserve was about eight miles from the community of Hope, where I had first met her years earlier, and about five miles from my father's farm. Knowing she was so close to the places that shaped my early life sparked something in me, a quiet reminder of how deeply her presence had once anchored me. She and Sister Yvonne lived next to the church on the reserve, continuing their work with the same steady presence.

In 2000, I made a calendar for Sister John with photos of my family. I had not seen her in a while, and I thought it would be a thoughtful gift. I wanted her to know that despite everything, she was still part of my story.

In the fall of 2001, I decided to visit Sister John and make a donation to support their little church. I gave her $500.00. She asked, "Do you want this to go to our community or to the church?"

"I want it to go to the church," I replied.

"Okay," she said.

A few months later, I received a thank-you card signed by her and the parishioners, along with a receipt for the charitable donation. I was touched. I had not received any cards from her in years. During a painful time in our relationship, I had even returned all the letters she had written to me. It felt like giving back pieces of my own heart, but I thought it was what she wanted. I believed she no longer wished to reach out, so I let them go.

Later that November, my mom, and I took a trip to Saskatchewan to visit Sisters Yvonne and John. While it was nice to see them both, I always felt uneasy when Sister John and my mom were together. Their presence created a tension I could not quite explain. It felt as if two parts of my life collided, one from my past and one from my pain, and I didn't know how to hold both.

During our stay, my mom and I visited a few others in the area. One evening, I left her at the sisters' house to visit Sister Yvonne. Sister John was out doing house visits, and I stepped out for a bit before returning later that night.

When I arrived, my mom said, "Sister Yvonne said we can stay overnight."

"What?" I replied. "I don't think that's a good idea."

Sister Yvonne reassured me, "It will be okay. You're one of Sister John's students."

But I hesitated. "I'm not sure Sister John is going to like this," I said, uncomfortably. It seemed Sister Yvonne did not fully understand the complicated history between us.

Despite my hesitation, Sister Yvonne insisted. My mom and I went downstairs to get ready for bed. Shortly after, Sister John returned and came downstairs. "What's going on?" she asked. I explained the situation, and to my surprise she simply said, "That's okay."

The next morning, we shared breakfast with Sisters Yvonne and John before returning to Calgary. There was a quiet peace in that moment, a sense that things were softening between us.

Later that year, I suggested to my friend Darlene that we go to Saskatchewan for Christmas. I wanted to visit my dad and attend midnight mass at the Bounty Reserve. We called my dad's girlfriend, Louise, who agreed to join us. I had no idea Louise knew Sister John, but I was not surprised. Small communities hold many connections. Louise told me, "Sister John has talked about you and how much she admired you." I was surprised to hear she still spoke of me so fondly after everything.

When we arrived at the church, Sister John addressed the parishioners and said, "Shelley Fraser is the one who gave us a donation to purchase chalices for the church. Shelley, please stand." As I rose, I felt seen, not just for what I gave, but for who I was. The parishioners applauded. She added, "We were hoping they would have arrived, but they haven't yet." Later that evening, she gave me a small statue of Joseph and Mary. I called her the next day and left a message saying, "It's beautiful."

After midnight mass, I gave Sisters John and Yvonne Christmas gifts. We stepped into a separate room, and with Louise and Darlene beside me, we watched Sister John open the gifts with childlike excitement, tearing into the packaging with pure joy. She asked if we would be around the next day.

"I'm not sure," I said. She thanked us warmly before we left.

Something had shifted in her. Her communication was clearer and more heartfelt than it had been in years. I was deeply moved. It reminded me that even strained relationships can find their way back to grace, one word or one gesture at a time. I came to realize how powerful communication can be, and how much it can shape, strain, or strengthen relationships.

As the new millennium unfolded, I began to understand that resilience was not only about enduring pain or seeking grace. It was about stepping into the future with a clearer sense of who I was and what I was meant to give.

The Morning I Walked Her Home

Chapter Eighteen
Parish Work

By 2002, I felt a growing desire to contribute more to the little parish where Sister John was staying. Giving had always been my way of staying connected to people, places, and purpose. Even when relationships were complicated, service felt simple.

That spring, I organized small auctions and bake sales at the Royal Canadian Legion in Calgary to raise funds for the church. When Darlene and I arrived at the Bounty Reserve, we brought Sisters John and Yvonne a donation of over $1,000.00, along with a cake and cards signed by those who supported the fundraiser. Their gratitude reminded me that generosity could bridge gaps that words sometimes could not.

During this time, Sister John would call my dad's farm and speak to his girlfriend, Louise, asking when I might be coming down for a visit. I found it odd that she asked through Louise rather than directly, but it revealed something important. Even in silence, she still wanted to know.

That spring, Sister Yvonne was preparing to leave for a short time. I brought her a vibrant bouquet of flowers. I admired her. She was pleasant, approachable, and deeply dedicated to her vocation. Her presence always carried calm.

One Sunday after church, Sister John asked me to come forward. She handed me a large photo of President Kennedy in a brown envelope. She knew I was fond of the Kennedy family, as I had visited Cape Cod. That same day, I had given her another donation, and she seemed pleasantly surprised. I had also purchased a sign for the church so the sisters could post announcements. To this day, the sign remains, a small legacy of my care.

That summer, I brought several items to the manager of the old convent, clocks, phones, and other things to help with the business. Sisters John and Yvonne later visited him, and he showed them what I had given. Sister John asked, "Why is there so much?" I did not know whether she was overwhelmed or simply curious. I had lived in that convent as a girl, and staying there again felt familiar, a quiet return to something I once knew.

Later that summer, Sister John and I had a disagreement. She sometimes said things that were hurtful without realizing it. I walked out of the sisters' house thinking, if you are going to insult me, I am not going to put up with it. That evening, I saw her drive into town with a new sister. She looked upset, surprised that I had walked out, and perhaps later realized she shouldn't have said what she did.

The next day, I returned. Still upset, I said, "I want my things back that I gave you."

She replied, "I wasn't trying to hurt you, and I wasn't done speaking."

As I turned to leave, she asked, "Is the candle still burning?"

"Yeah, I guess so… I don't know," I said, and walked out. With Sister John, it was often hard to understand what she truly meant. Once again, I found myself trying to grasp and express the meaning behind her words.

That fall, a new priest arrived, Father George. He served both the church in Hope and the Bounty Reserve. He was from Africa, approachable, kind, and easy to talk to. I spoke with him often and visited whenever I was around. My friend Darlene liked him too. They always had thoughtful conversations.

One day, I asked if the church needed anything.

"Our computer isn't working," he said.

"Okay," I replied. "Let me see what we can do."

I purchased a computer for the church. Father George and the parish secretary were delighted, and word spread through the church bulletin. Sister John attended that church during the week, as reserve services were held only on Sundays.

Later that fall, I received a receipt from Sister John for the $1,000.00, but she had listed only my first name and Darlene's.

"This will not do," I said. I left a message asking for it to be redone.

She called back and said, "I cannot change it." Later that month, I attended church and brought her a book explaining how receipts should be issued. I gently left it on the counter and said, "Here is the book regarding receipts." She grew angry and said, "I've had enough." I wasn't sure what she meant, so I left. Darlene tried to speak with her but got nowhere. Eventually, Sister Yvonne intervened and said, "I'll call Sister John now and get her to change it." The matter was resolved.

Christmas arrived, and I attended midnight mass at the Bounty Reserve. I did not speak to Sister John, but when I entered the church, the new sister waved me over and found me a seat. After mass, I left gifts for Sister John on the counter, including a small pillow with a pocket for a rosary.

A few days later, while staying at the old convent, I returned from Prince Albert and realized I had passed the sisters' vehicle on the highway. When I got back to town, I saw that they had picked up their mail. Later, I noticed Sister John's vehicle looping around the school and the convent. I wondered if she was checking to see if my car was there.

In 2003, while I was resting, Darlene brought me a box. "You have a parcel," she said. She did not recognize the handwriting. I did.

"Oh, it's from Sister John," I said.

The parcel read, "These are being returned to you before you ask for them back." It had several stamps. I laughed. I was not hurt. It was her way of speaking without saying she was angry but still thinking of me. For someone who did not want the gifts, she had put a great deal of effort into wrapping them, writing a note, and preparing the package. I knew immediately she was upset, likely hurt.

Darlene called Father George, who said, "This is serious…"

I told him, "No. She's just upset with me."

The Morning I Walked Her Home

He later added, "Every time I mentioned your name, Sister John appeared to have an angry look on her face. But I know she does love you." He also said that Sister John had remarked, "I know Shelley will be angry about the return of the gifts."

Months later, she eventually received the rosary pillow I had given her, one of the gifts she had returned.

As time passed, I decided to return to Saskatchewan. I moved back to the small community where I had helped both churches. Every corner held echoes of who I had been and who I was becoming. I expected it to be difficult, surrounded by memories of pain, yet I felt more at ease this time and enjoyed being involved in both churches. Even so, I never felt fully relaxed. I was likely living with unresolved post-traumatic stress disorder, but I never had the guidance or therapy I needed to understand those feelings.

I helped the Hope community with fundraising activities. Though I kept my distance from most people, I still found ways to contribute quietly. My instinct to withdraw was rooted in a deep need for safety, but I refused to let pain define me. Even while avoiding close connections, I chose small acts that reminded me I still had something to offer. These moments of guarded involvement became my path toward healing, my way of rising above the weight of my past without exposing myself to further hurt.

In May, I visited Father George and asked if there was anything my friend and I could do for the church. Helping gave me a way to stay connected without getting too close.

"Yes," he said. "We need our basement church windows renovated."

"Okay," I replied. "Let's see what we can do."

My friend Cecile and I organized a silent auction in the church basement, collecting items from local businesses. The event included entertainment, refreshments, and more.

To my surprise, Sister John and the new sister attended the fundraiser. Even though we did not speak, her presence felt like a quiet acknowledgment, as if she were still watching from the edges. Cecile and I let the parish council run the event. At the end of the evening, the council president asked if I had anything to say.

"I just want to thank everyone for coming out," I said simply.

Everyone stood and applauded. I thanked Cecile as well.

Later that summer, the Bounty Reserve held a garage sale at the church. I did not attend, but I sent an envelope with friends and asked them to give it to Sister John. Even when I kept my distance, I still wanted to support her work. It was my way of saying; I am still here. Later that day, Sister John called the convent manager to share how much they had raised, and he relayed the message to me.

That fall, I spoke to Father George about painting the church.

"I'll check and get some estimates," he said.

Yet Sister John began asking about the project. She asked Father George, "I hear Shelley wants to paint the church."

"We're trying to get estimates," he told her.

She did not ask me directly. It was her way of staying close without crossing the line. It often felt like she was always around in some quiet way, finding out what I was up to.

As I reflect now, I realize Sister John's actions were never about indifference. She cared, but she carried that care in ways I did not always understand. Sometimes it came through silence, other times through indirect questions, and at moments through gestures that felt contradictory, like returning gifts yet wrapping them with care, asking about me through others, or watching quietly from the edges of a room.

For me, it often felt confusing and even hurtful. Beneath it all was a connection she could not name and one I could not let go. Her restraint was not a lack of love but the weight of boundaries she struggled to uphold. And though her words were few, her presence told me I mattered.

The Morning I Walked Her Home

Chapter Nineteen
Faith, Fundraisers, and the Flying Bun

By 2004 my life had become a balancing act between service, solitude, connection, and caution. That fall I finally made the decision to stay with the Bounty Reserve parish where Sister John was. I chose to remain with her parish rather than continue at the small community of Hope. Around the same time Sister Yvonne returned from her leave, and for a while everything seemed to be going smoothly.

In the early winter of that year, I was involved in a car accident at the Bounty Reserve. The other driver did not have insurance, and my car was sideswiped. Thankfully I was not badly hurt. I left a message for Sisters John and Yvonne to let them know what had happened. Sister John later called the manager of the old convent to ask how I was. A day or two later both sisters came to the convent after morning mass to visit, but I was asleep and missed them.

When I woke and went upstairs the manager handed me a small gift, a magnet showing two angels with a heart in the middle. "Sister left this for you," he said. It felt like a quiet gesture of care, something she could not say out loud but still wanted me to feel. Later at church I thanked Sister John and asked her to thank Sister Yvonne as well. Sister John simply said, "I was the one who gave it to you." I replied, "Oh, okay, thank you," and quietly walked away.

Fundraising quickly became my focus. I would go to surrounding communities to collect items for silent auctions. Asking local businesses for support came easily to me, but the sisters had little experience with raising money. My friend Joe came with me to one of the parish fundraisers and was shocked to see prizes being given away for twenty-five cents a ticket or five for a dollar. "That is a god damn giveaway," he exclaimed. I agreed. Brand new coffee pots worth thirty dollars or more were being handed out for almost nothing.

Eventually I told Sister John, "You need to increase the cost of your tickets, otherwise you won't make any money." I believe the sisters feared that asking too much would discourage people from supporting the parish, but the community was willing. Joe would often tease, "You're hers," referring to Sister John. I laughed it off, but deep down I knew there was some truth in it, not in a possessive way but in the quiet affection she had carried for me over the years.

One day Sister John commented that others would probably get upset with me because of her. It was a strange thing to hear, yet it revealed how aware she was of the tension she carried with people at the Bounty Reserve. When conflicts arose around her, the frustration often spilled over onto me, even when I had nothing to do with the situation. Her remark stayed with me, a quiet acknowledgment that I was sometimes caught in the crossfire of her relationships with others.

Later that November my friend Loretta at the reserve often hosted bingos for the community, and I would occasionally help her. One evening I was surprised to see Sisters John and Yvonne walk into the bingo hall. Sister John immediately headed to the kitchen where Loretta was. As I stood nearby, she said, "I hear you have been saying some things about us sisters." Then she turned to me and added, "Shelley, you stay out of this." Loretta calmly replied, "Well Sister, it is none of your business what I do at my bingos." The sisters left shortly after.

Not long after there was another parish fundraiser. I had brought many donated items from local businesses. When Sister John auctioned them off, she would say things like, "This is Shelley's milk or bread, how much do you want to pay for it?" It felt uncomfortable to be singled out like that, as though my contributions needed to be highlighted.

In April of 2005 I was involved in another car accident in Calgary. A man fleeing a helicopter police chase had stolen a vehicle, sped through a red light downtown, hit my car, and spun me around in a full circle. His vehicle then bounced off another car driven by a pregnant woman. I later checked to be sure she was okay and thankfully she was. I did not suffer major injuries, but my car was totaled. At the time I was serving as president of the Ladies' Auxiliary of the Royal

Canadian Legion, and I was also the youngest elected auxiliary president in Calgary that year.

In the early winter of 2006, the sisters hosted entertainment at the church and I attended. When Elvis Presley's "Cannot Help Falling in Love" played on the CD player, Sister John pointed it out to me. She did not say a word, but the meaning in her gesture lingered.

That spring Sisters John and Yvonne held another event at the church. Joe and I went but did not stay long. I told Joe, "Give this box of items to the sisters, they can use it for their next fundraiser." Joe handed the box to Sister Yvonne while Sister John was cutting a bun. Joe later told me she had said, "I need to talk to that girl," referring to me.

Joe left the building first and waited in the car. A moment later Sister John approached while I was sitting with him. She spoke briefly but said little, likely because Joe was there with me. Over time she began calling me at Joe's house. One day when we arrived at church Joe suddenly said he did not want to attend anymore. I left Sister John a message explaining we would not be coming. She called back and spoke to Joe, who only said, "I have my reasons."

There was another time when I visited Pat at her home. Sisters John and Yvonne happened to be there when I arrived. I did not sit at the table with them. Instead, I stood near the deep freeze in the hallway while visiting Pat and her grandchildren. As Sister John passed me on her way to the washroom, she gently squeezed my arm and said, "I am jealous." Her words hung in the air, unexpected, vulnerable, and strangely tender.

Later that winter Sister John rolled the sisters' vehicle after hitting an icy patch. Their Jeep was totaled. Pat called me at Joe's to tell me Sister John had been in an accident. My first question was simple. "Is Sister John okay?" Pat reassured me that she was shaken but safe.

The Morning I Walked Her Home

A gift from Sister John to Shelley after an accident at the
Bounty Reserve.

Shelley Fraser

Chapter Twenty
The Road Between Two Worlds

In the early winter of 2007, my friend Joe and I decided to raise money for Sister John's parish. One day, Joe went to the post office and picked up a large envelope. The following Sunday, he and I went to church together. As you may recall, Joe did not want to return to the church, but he made an exception for this.

We had placed the donation in the envelope. When we arrived, I walked in and handed it to Sister John, saying, "This is for the church." She responded, "Okay," and carried it to the front. After Mass ended, Sister John was visibly excited. As she often did, she stood at the front and announced, "The good-looking couple in the back just gave us a donation of $1,000.00." I knew exactly who she meant. I grinned at Joe, but he remained expressionless.

Later that winter, the sisters, my friend Pat, and I began hosting bingos in the community of Hope to raise money for the church. Pat and I met with the town council of Hope, and they agreed to let us hold them. The bingos benefited both parishes, Bounty Reserve and Hope. It was meaningful because Sister John and I worked side by side. We shared laughter, teasing, and a quiet understanding. For a time, it felt like healing was happening in the simplest ways.

A few months later, another fundraiser was held at the church. Joe suggested, "Have the sisters come over and pick up the stuff you have for them." Sister Yvonne arrived first, and I went out to help her load the items. As soon as Sister John saw me, she came out to assist as well. Joe frowned. "Why is Sister John sending poor little Sister Yvonne to come get the stuff?" I shrugged. The sisters thanked us and drove away.

Not long after, Sister Yvonne made a comment that caught me off guard. "I don't know what it is about you two," she said, referring to Sister John and me, "but you guys better keep it real." Then she added, "You know she loves you." Hearing it spoken aloud startled me.

I had always sensed something between us, but now it was undeniable.

One day, Sister John called and asked, "Would you like to visit the old convent with Sister Yvonne and me? It has new owners." She offered to pick me up, and I agreed. We visited together. The previous manager, Joe's older brother, had passed away. That convent was where Joe and I had first got to know each other. He was safe, kind, and respectful. He was my best friend.

In March, Sisters John, Yvonne, and Doris, along with Pat, invited me out for my birthday. We met at a local restaurant for supper, and I sat beside Sister John. The sisters gave me birthday cards, one signed by all three, and another from Sister John personally. Her card read in French, "Une amie extraordinaire," meaning "An extraordinary friend." It was thoughtful, and I was touched that they remembered.

Later that spring, Pat called. "Sister John is going to be leaving the reserve," she said. I was surprised she was the one telling me. Then she added, "Sister wanted me to tell you because she knew you'd be upset." Sister John had served at the Bounty Reserve for eight years. We shared laughter, healing, and countless parish events. I was disappointed to hear she would be leaving.

But I had plans of my own. A new priest, Father Vince, had arrived. During a visit to the rectory, he asked if I would be interested in teaching English in Uganda. I told him I needed time to think. That evening, I called him back and said yes.

Soon after, I called the sisters to share the news. "I'm going to Africa," I told Sisters John and Yvonne. I believe Sister John was surprised. At one gathering she said, "When I'm in Prince Albert, you can come work with me…" I replied, "You know I would." She laughed softly. "I know you would."

In May, we held a fundraiser for Father Vince to support a school in Uganda. That evening, we raised over $1,000.00. Sisters John and Yvonne were present. A few weeks later, another fundraiser was organized to support my upcoming trip to Africa.

The Morning I Walked Her Home

Soon after, Sister John called me at Joe's. "Would you be interested in doing an interview for the *Prairie Messenger* about your trip to Uganda?" she asked. I agreed, and the Catholic newspaper published the interview a few weeks later.

Later that month, I phoned the sisters' house at the reserve. Sister John answered. I asked, "May I speak to Sister Doris?" She sounded surprised that I had asked for Doris instead of her. When I arrived, Sister Doris welcomed me, and both Sisters John and Yvonne were at the table. We played cards, Sisters Doris and Yvonne as partners, and Sister John and I together. Sister John grew slightly annoyed. I was not sure why. Perhaps she was hurt, jealous, or simply tired. Something had shifted. I left quickly, sensing tension.

By June, things were winding down. I spoke with Sister Yvonne and said, "We have to do something special for Sister John before she leaves for Prince Albert." She agreed. I gathered cards and had people from the reserve sign them. I bought a cake and a briefcase with a nameplate and filled it with small gifts. I created a poster filled with photos of Sister John, images from her years of service at the Bounty Reserve and some from her earlier teaching years. I think she was shocked to see so many pictures of herself, a tribute to both past and present.

One day after Mass, Sister John surprised me. She stood at the front of the church and spoke about me. She had written down some things that she wanted to share with the parishioners. The sisters presented me with a cake, a beautiful card, and a heartfelt write-up. Then, to my astonishment, they gave me a large plaque. I was deeply moved. The respect, care, and love between Sister John and me felt mutual. It wasn't always easy, but it was real. She had a way of putting me on a pedestal, and I did the same for her.

The following Sunday, Sister John and I were invited to lunch by a parishioner. I drove, and we spent a few hours visiting before I took her back to the house at the Bounty Reserve.

Shelley Fraser

Chapter Twenty-One
Uganda

In August, I arrived in Uganda after a long flight from Canada. It was dark when I landed, and everything felt unfamiliar. I was given the priest's room to sleep in, and after calling Sister John to let her know I had arrived, I slept for nearly two days.

When I finally woke up, the heat and the sound of unfamiliar birds greeted me. I went for a walk to explore. The buildings looked different from those back home, and even the animals were slender compared to the ones I was used to, such as the cat and dog I saw. I passed a building full of corn and met the seminarians. We spent days shelling corn until my hands grew calloused. When classes began, we struggled with each other's accents, but eventually we found our rhythm.

I collaborated with another sister from the United States who taught psychology. One memory that stands out is shelling peanuts for days, tedious yet oddly satisfying. The days were hot, but by seven in the evening the air cooled. When it rained, the roads became slick, and the diesel fumes often made me sick. I saw people carrying heavy jugs of water on bicycles, working with little machinery, and selling what they could to earn a small income. Some asked me for help with school fees. I even saw animals living inside homes, including a full-grown pig. The suffering around me made me realize how much we take for granted in Canada.

At a hospital, a young girl with polio took my hand and walked with me. It was a moment I will never forget.

Sister John and I mostly communicated by email. She wrote often, sometimes twice a week. In her first message she asked, "Have you started preparing your classes? I'd love to be a birdie able to peek in your window!"

A week later she wrote again, "Hope to hear from you soon. Still would like to be a little birdie in Uganda to peep into your classes." Her words were playful and warm.

Life was not easy. One day the village lost power and water. After several days, I asked the priest, "If I lend you the money, could you get the power and water working again?" He said yes.

During this time, one of my students became extremely ill with typhoid fever, but thankfully he recovered. The seminarians were also growing weary; they often complained that the priest was overworking them. With everything feeling strained, I eventually decided to move to an orphanage down the hill. It had empty residences and a generator, so I still had electricity during outages.

One day, Sister John called and asked how things were going. "They're going," I said. She gently told me, "You don't need to stay there if you don't want to." I told her I would stick it out.

Later, she emailed asking, "Are you coming for Christmas? Llllllong time no see!" I did not answer. Instead, I surprised her by showing up at the Diocese office. When she saw me, she was thrilled. We went to the "Big House" for lunch, and one of the sisters took a photo of us.

Later that week, she called and asked if I would pick her up so we could attend Mass together in Prince Albert, and we did.

It felt wonderful to be back in Canada, though I often found myself comparing our comforts to the hardships I had seen in Africa. My mom had moved from Calgary to Saskatchewan, so I visited her during the holidays. Joe was happy to see me too, and I shared my experiences with him.

As I carried the memories of Sister John's care and the lessons of Uganda with me, I realized my journey had become more than survival or service. It was about weaving together two worlds, the one I had left and the one I had stepped into.

Sister John and Shelley having lunch in 2007 at the "Big House," during Shelley's Christmas visit from Uganda; Sister John's rosary, later given to Shelley, lies to the right.

Shelley Fraser

89

Chapter Twenty-Two
From Saskatchewan to Uganda

In early 2008, I felt an ardent desire to give back to Uganda. Time was short, but I organized a toy drive. The local newspaper featured a story, the radio station promoted it, and a store agreed to collect donations. The community's response was overwhelming. Due to airline restrictions, I couldn't take all the toys with me, but the generosity of the community reminded me how deeply people care when given the opportunity. It felt like a small miracle.

Before returning to Uganda, I visited Sister John at the "Big House." She brought down some of the other sisters to greet me. I had stayed with some of them back in 1980 and seeing them again was heartwarming. It felt as though time had folded in on itself, carrying me back to those early years.

Upon my return to Africa, I purchased T-shirts for the seminarians. They were grateful, and I handed out the extras to the workers. However, one day I was shocked to discover rats in my duffle bag. While searching for my cell phone, I noticed shredded paper inside. Startled, I asked my students to remove the bag the following day. I informed Sister John about what had happened, and she emailed me, saying, "Your things are replaceable." Since then, I have been terrified of rodents.

In February, Sister John emailed again, mentioning she had spoken to my mom. I was surprised she had reached out. "Shelley, I spoke to your mom. She wanted to call you, but I told her it was very expensive. I tried calling a few times, but there was no answer." It meant a lot that she had reached out to my mom. It was one of those quiet gestures that conveyed, I am still here and I still care.

Sister John occasionally spoke to other priests, Father Vince, George, or Bob, inquiring about me and sharing updates on my experience in Africa. In March, I returned to Canada. Coming home was bittersweet.

Shelley Fraser

Chapter Twenty-Three
Purpose and Personal Strength

When I returned to Canada after my journey in Africa, I carried more than memories; I carried a mission. Visiting schools and delivering supplies to children had affected me deeply, and I wanted to do more. That was when the idea for the Provincial Bike Athlon came to mind, a fundraising trek across Saskatchewan to support students in Africa.

Organizing the event took time, effort, and the generosity of many. We held community barbecues and bingo nights, and people and businesses gave with open hearts. Sister John joined us at one of the barbecues in Prince Albert, and Pat helped too. Others pitched in by driving vehicles, arranging meals, and securing places to stay. Sister John contributed quietly, reminding me of how she would always show up without seeking recognition. Her presence meant more than she realized.

I reached out to parishes across the province, sending flyers and letters. Many parishioners responded with heartfelt donations. To further support the cause, I sold copies of my book *Unexpected Guests*, which shared my story from Africa. It was available at a local beverage store, and all proceeds went toward the fundraiser.

At the end of June 2008, I began the 2,000-kilometre bike trek. It was a summer of purpose, but also of personal hardship. My mother had begun feeling unwell. During visits, I noticed troubling signs of blood in her washroom. Despite having home care, her condition had been overlooked. I urged her to see a doctor. Initially, she was told she needed a hysterectomy, but further tests in Saskatoon revealed something far more serious, colon cancer.

The prognosis was devastating. Mom had six to nine months at most. She began radiation treatments, and I drove her to every appointment. I asked how she felt about everything, but she said little. Perhaps she was quietly coming to terms with reality.

Shelley Fraser

In August, I learned that a friend of mine had lost her husband after a lengthy illness. His wife was a cousin of Sister John. The funeral was held in the small community where I had spent some weekends with her as a teenager. I attended and saw Sisters Yvonne and Doris. I wasn't expecting Sister John, but she was there. After the service, Sister Doris handed me the keys and said, "You can drive us to the cemetery." I agreed. As I sat in the driver's seat of the sisters' Jeep, I saw Sister John walk past us on the sidewalk. At the time, she was staying at the "Big House" in Prince Albert.

Shortly after, I returned to Prince Albert to check on Sister John. By the look on her face, I could tell she wasn't happy. I sensed she was upset about me being with the other sisters. Maybe she felt left out. Maybe seeing me with them troubled her. Her silence spoke louder than words ever could.

Later that summer, at Saskatoon City Hospital, I unexpectedly spotted Sister John looking at a vehicle. It was mine. I asked, "What are you doing here?" I explained I had brought my mom to see the doctor. She introduced me to her brother and sister-in-law. It was unexpected but comforting. Even in a place filled with worry, her presence brought familiarity. It reminded me that some connections endure, even when everything else feels uncertain. We kept in touch occasionally by phone.

In September, the Royal Canadian Legion honored me with a plaque for my work as Ladies' Auxiliary president. I was surprised when someone asked, "Did you receive your plaque?" I hadn't expected anything in return for my service, and the recognition felt meaningful.

Later that month, during one of Sister John's rounds as a spiritual director in Saskatoon, she visited my mom's room. Mom, who was sharing the space with another patient, said, "Sister John has known my daughter Shelley ever since she was a young girl." Sister John didn't stay long. Perhaps it was too emotional, or she didn't know what to say. But her presence, even for a moment, was a quiet acknowledgment of the years we had shared.

The Morning I Walked Her Home

Despite Mom's illness, in October she wanted to return to the community of Hope, where she had lived with my dad and had us four children. She spent a few months there, walking through town despite her condition, still strong in spirit.

Mom spent one final Christmas with her sister Jenny before moving to a care home, where she remained until her passing in May 2009.

As I faced the loss of my mother and the shifting presence of Sister John, I began to understand that my journey was no longer just about service or survival. It was about learning how love, faith, and resilience could guide me through grief in whatever came next.

Shelley's book, dedicated to Sister John in 2008.

The Morning I Walked Her Home

Chapter Twenty-Four
The Year of Mom's Passing

In early 2009, I enrolled in a heavy equipment course and successfully completed it. At the time, my mom was living in a care home, and I visited her whenever I could. Watching her suffering was heartbreaking. Staying busy helped me cope, though the weight of her illness was always present.

In March, her sister Jenny organized a birthday party for Mom at the care home. It was a lovely gathering. Jenny often stayed with Mom and played music for her. During that time, I felt defeated and uncertain about my own future. I was stuck, unsure which direction to take. Sometimes I spoke to Mom out of frustration, but deep down, I was grappling with the reality that her life was drawing to a close.

Occasionally, I visited Sisters Yvonne and Doris at the Bounty Reserve, but it wasn't the same without Sister John. Her absence was palpable, in the quiet spaces, in the way the room didn't light up, in the grounding presence I had always relied on.

In early May, I received a call from the home care staff telling me Mom's condition had worsened and that I should come immediately. When I arrived, I could sense that death was near. Her sister Jenny and other family members were already there. I sat beside Mom and spoke to her. Though she didn't respond, I could tell she understood. Her eyes opened briefly, and I thought she might say something, but she remained silent. I gently told her, "Mom, it's going to be okay. You can go now and spend time with your other daughter." Soon after, Mom took her final breath. She passed away the day before Mother's Day, on May 9, 2009. She was 58. I held her in my arms and cried. She had brought me into this world, and now I had witnessed her leaving it. It felt surreal.

Mom had endured a difficult life, and in her later years, she struggled with mental health issues. My brother Stewart and his wife arrived, and we stayed until the funeral home came to take her.

The Morning I Walked Her Home

Later that day, I spoke with Sister John and told her Mom had passed. She called back a few times to offer guidance and suggestions for the funeral. My brother and I decided on cremation. Sister John kindly offered to do a reading, and she stood beside me when I did mine.

The funeral was held in Prince Albert at the Sacred Heart Cathedral, the same place where my grandmother's service had been years earlier. Sister John drove from Saskatoon to attend. Mom's family and friends were present, including our dad, the sisters from Bounty Reserve, and my friend Joe. After the service, we had lunch together. The weather was beautiful, as if the sky had opened in grace, offering a sense of peace after so much pain.

After the funeral, my brothers and I visited the cemetery where our baby sister was buried. We placed the remaining flowers at her grave. Our dad waited for us at a local bar, but we chose to go our separate ways.

I kept Mom's ashes for a short time. I wrote her a letter and placed it in the box Joe and I had built. Together, we drove to the cemetery and buried the remains. Later, Sisters Yvonne and Doris joined me to bless Mom's grave.

As I reflected on Mom's life, I remembered how much she loved music. When she was married to our dad, her friends would tell me years later that they could hear her music playing across the railroad tracks in Hope as they stepped out of their vehicles to shop at the grocery store. One friend said, "That must be Barbara playing Elvis Presley." Music ran in our family. Perhaps listening to it was her way of coping with the struggles at home.

Grief did not disappear, but it softened. I needed purpose, and the church gave me a place to pour my energy. That fall, I returned to the Bounty Reserve parish and helped organize another fundraiser. The sisters let me take the lead, as they did not have much experience with fundraising. We raised over $3,000.00 and the turnout was wonderful. People came from surrounding communities.

After the fundraiser, I sat down with Sisters Yvonne and Doris as they counted the money. I teased Sister Doris, saying, "You forgot to count the money we brought in." She replied, "Well, you can live with it…" The next day, I called her and asked, "Do you want me to come over with the fundraiser money?" She said yes. When I arrived, I was wearing one of Joe's jackets with many pockets. I joked, "Which pocket do you want me to pull the money out of?" They both laughed and picked one. Things were going well, and I enjoyed helping the parish.

One day, a woman from a nearby community said, "Shelley, if it weren't for you, that church wouldn't survive." I took it as a kind compliment, though I always remained humble about such praise.

That fall, I also had shoulder surgery for an injury sustained while working in Prince Albert. My friend Joe accompanied me to Saskatoon for surgery. It was the first of several I would need, and his support meant a great deal.

In November, it was Sister Doris's birthday. I bought her a gift and brought pizza for the three of us to enjoy. She thanked me for the beautiful day. Shortly after, Sister Doris and I had a small disagreement, but a few days later, at a church function, we hugged and made up. It was our way of apologizing. Sister Yvonne often said, "I know when the two of you hurt each other, you always hug afterward."

As 2009 came to a close, the sisters and I shared supper together. I brought Christmas gifts, and they gave me a gift and card in return. As the year ended, I felt a quiet sense of healing. Loss had marked the year, but through it all, the sisters remained a steady light.

As I stepped out of the shadow of grief, I realized that loss had reshaped me, but it had also deepened my resolve to keep serving, to keep building, and to keep finding light in the places where darkness had lingered.

The Morning I Walked Her Home

Shelley Fraser

Chapter Twenty-Five
Spiritual Burnout and Betrayal

By 2010, I felt a deep need for change. The routine I had grown accustomed to was wearing thin, and my role in the church had become narrowly focused on fundraising. It seemed as though my worth was measured only by how much money I could raise, and that realization weighed heavily on me. I began to feel invisible, as if the person I was beyond my contributions mattered less than the funds I brought in for the parish.

That spring, I reached out to two retired Catholic sisters who had once lived in Ontario and were now residing in Prince Albert. I called them, and eventually they returned my call. I asked if they could use some help, and they welcomed my offer. I began assisting them wherever support was needed. These women were intelligent and wise, and I genuinely enjoyed listening to their stories and insights. Being around them reminded me of the deeper sense of purpose I had once felt.

During this time, I continued attending church at the Bounty Reserve. While staying with the sisters in Prince Albert, I also underwent physiotherapy for my shoulder. Together, we visited nearby reserves and occasionally attended diocesan meetings. At these gatherings, I would sometimes see Sisters Yvonne and Doris. I also stayed connected with Sister John in Saskatoon, occasionally meeting her at the house for lunch or going out for supper.

Tensions began to rise between Sister Doris and me at the Bounty Reserve. Things came to a head one night in October. I proposed a fundraiser and suggested that fifty percent of the proceeds go to a new hospital being built about sixty kilometers away. I felt this was fair, especially since I had contributed most of the items for the event. Sister Doris said she would consult the parish council, and they agreed that a portion of the proceeds could go to the hospital.

Before the fundraiser took place, I was involved in a car accident. It happened on a dark Monday night while driving to a church service at the Bounty Reserve. As we approached a hill, we did not see the wild horses on the road. One was struck, injuring it and shattering my windshield. Despite the damage, my car was still drivable. I suffered a concussion and a jaw injury, but we still attended the service and returned to Hope afterward. I was shaken, not just physically but emotionally. It felt as though life was trying to slow me down, to force me to confront what I had been pushing through.

The fundraiser eventually went ahead and was a success. Afterward, I suggested to Sister Doris that we donate $500.00 instead of the original $700.00 to $750.00 In hindsight, my concussion likely affected my judgment. The next day, I called her to ask when I could pick up the cheque. To my surprise, she hesitated and claimed the hospital was no longer accepting donations. I knew this wasn't true. What organization turns down a donation? It wasn't just about the money. It was about trust, about feeling that the values I held dear, such as generosity, honesty, and service, were being quietly dismissed.

Other troubling signs appeared. Once, I placed a $50.00 bill in the collection plate and later asked Sister Yvonne if she had received it. She said she hadn't, and I believed her. The only people handling the plate were Sisters Yvonne and Doris. I began to feel that Sister Doris might not be trustworthy with money. I had been donating regularly to the church, but eventually I stopped because I no longer felt confident that the funds were being used appropriately.

Thinking back, I regret lowering the hospital donation amount. When someone suffers a concussion, judgment can be impaired. Sister Doris should have recognized that and honored the original figure. Her actions did not add up, and I felt she had taken advantage of people's generosity. In the end, I did receive the cheque, though she gave it reluctantly.

Later that December, I spoke with Sister John in Saskatoon. She had previously expressed that the Bounty Reserve needed to learn to raise its own funds and was not supportive of my continued fundraising efforts there. I also told her about the car accident, and she showed genuine concern.

That month, I met Sister John again in Saskatoon and gave her a Christmas card. On it, I wrote "30 years of knowing each other."

Another afternoon, I took her out for supper. As I dropped her off, she made a comment that caught me off guard. Her words were brief but carried weight. I do not remember exactly what she said, only how it made me feel, as though something had shifted, as if the closeness we shared was beginning to fade. Little did she and I know this would be the last time we would speak to each other.

The Morning I Walked Her Home

Chapter Twenty-Six
Right from the Heart

In 2011, I decided to author another book, *Right from the Heart*. Before its release, I called Sister John once that year. She was now living at the "Big House" in Prince Albert. During our conversation, she asked, "I thought you were teaching in Saudi Arabia…" Her voice felt distant, as though we were speaking across a quiet emotional divide. I realized we were no longer walking the same path.

I had indeed signed a contract to teach at a university there, but my doctor advised against it. She said I was not well enough because of the concussion and injuries from the car accident.

Right from the Heart was deeply personal. It reflected on the loss of my mother, the experiences I had endured, and the emotional challenges I faced. Writing has always been therapeutic for me. It allows me to share my journey and remind others that they are not alone in their healing. Each page was a release, a way to honor what I had lost and reclaim what I still carried. The book was not only about grieving those who had passed. It was also about the emotional loss of people who are still present in our lives. When relationships change, we must adjust, just as we do when we lose someone to death.

When the book was released in November 2011, the local newspaper featured a large article on it. The book sold well, and Coles Bookstore requested additional copies. I donated some of the proceeds to help the Bounty Reserve with food hampers for Christmas.

Throughout 2011, I continued attending church at the Bounty Reserve and remained involved in fundraising, but my enthusiasm had waned. The trust I once had in Sister Doris was broken, and I knew it was only a matter of time before I began to step back.

One incident stood out. I confronted Sister Doris about how she had taken advantage of me, especially regarding fundraising. She became angry and told me to leave the house. She also said, "I have no right to kick anybody out of the parish as it is a public place." That comment lingered with me. It made me realize she had considered doing just that. The place I once called sacred had become a space of control and silence. No one has the authority to ask someone to leave a church. It is a public space, and that kind of behavior is a form of spiritual abuse, exploiting someone for personal gain and belittling them when it comes to matters of faith.

That year, the church held several seminars for parishioners. I attended, hoping they would be meaningful. One evening, Sister Yvonne stood up and said, "I am glad Shelley came back. I wanted to tell you myself, but I was afraid I would cry." Her voice trembled with sincerity. In that moment, I felt seen, not for what I could give, but for who I was. Her words touched me deeply. Sister Yvonne was a woman of true faith. She was the longest serving sister at the Bounty Reserve and was respected by many, including myself. She accepted people as they were and never sought personal gain. She was a helper to many.

One day, Sister Wendy gently told me, "You may need to step away from these sisters, because it is becoming unhealthy." I took her advice seriously and slowly began to distance myself. I started volunteering with other organizations, which brought new experiences and joy. The church began to feel less central in my life.

Later, I became more involved in the Bounty Reserve community itself, organizing food hampers, preparing goody bags for youth, raising money for the youth center, purchasing items for the care home, and donating to the local school for one of the graduates. My friend Irene played a significant role in this work, especially helping with bingos. Although she later passed, her support had been vital. Without her, we would not have helped as many people as we did.

By the end of 2011, I had written and released *Right from the Heart*. I also began slowly stepping back from church involvement and letting go of relationships that no longer felt healthy. It was a year of reflection, healing, and quiet transformation.

As I stepped back from the parish and poured my energy into new paths, I realized that the next chapter of my life would not be defined by betrayal or burnout. It would be shaped by the search for renewal, purpose, and a deeper kind of faith that could withstand change.

Some of these religious figures left a sour impression. It was disheartening. When I reflect on the young girl I once was, six or seven years old, full of belief and wonder, I realize the faith I once held had been eroded. The Catholic Church had lost some of its authenticity, not because of its teachings, but because of the behavior of its representatives. Many were emotionally wounded themselves, and their behavior risked negatively influencing others in the congregation.

I want to be clear that I am not criticizing those who continue to find meaning in their faith. Many good people still exist within the church. But it is hard to inspire others when the institution's reputation has been damaged by those entrusted to uphold it.

Shelley presenting a cheque to the Prince Albert Food Bank in 2011.

Shelley working on her book *Right from the Heart* in 2011.

Shelley Fraser

Chapter Twenty-Seven
Letting Go to Find Peace

In 2012, I occasionally assisted Sister Wendy with various tasks. One day, while helping at a function in the basement of a cathedral in Prince Albert, I noticed a woman I had worked with during bingo nights at the reserve. She recognized me, and we met near the back of the room, looking at posters on the wall.

Suddenly, I heard a familiar voice call my name, "Shelley, Shelley." The second time I heard it, I knew exactly who it was, Sister John. I didn't turn to acknowledge her. Instead, I quietly made my way out the door. I thought about going back but chose to keep walking. I was emotionally drained. That voice, once comforting, now carried fatigue, sadness, and the weight of too many unresolved moments. Dealing with some of the sisters had become exhausting, and I was done carrying that burden.

That same year, I became involved in fundraising for the sisters public swimming pool. The sisters at the "Big House" had opened their pool to the public but needed additional funds to keep it running. I partnered with a local funeral home, and together we organized a silent auction and lunch. I visited local businesses to collect items, and the event turned out to be a success.

I also helped with the Indigenous Winter Games and soon discovered that a lot of food had been left over. The staff told me, "Take whatever you want, most of it will go to waste anyway." My cousin Julie and I gathered the food, donating some to the YWCA, sharing some with families in need, and bringing some to the Bounty Reserve. The people were grateful.

In the spring, my mom's youngest sister, Jenny, passed away due to complications from diabetes. I was with her when she passed, holding her hand in those quiet final moments. Her funeral was held in Prince Albert. Afterward, my cousins gave me her ashes. They had scattered some at the cemetery on the hill, but the bag had a hole in it.

They said, "Jen was close to your mom, so you might as well take them and put them with her." I agreed. I made a small box with her name on it, wrote a letter, and buried her ashes near my mom's grave with my cousin Julie. Sister Wendy and Roy joined me for a quiet blessing.

2012 became a year of reflection, a time when I realized that change was necessary. By the end of summer, my perspective had shifted. The church no longer felt like home; it felt like a place I had outgrown. I didn't reach out to Sister John, and attending services no longer brought comfort. Church began to feel like a duty rather than a spiritual experience. Its meaning and purpose were fading. In retrospect, I see how easily someone generous can be taken advantage of.

Even now, people ask me about fundraising, and I tell them, "Those fundraising days are long over." Over the years, I noticed that many in positions of authority within the church often went on power trips. The truth is, they were no different from anyone else. One of the biggest issues was that no one really knew how to fundraise, not even the sisters. How could they lead parishioners when they could not guide them themselves?

Shelley with a friend at the Bounty Reserve celebrating
Saskatchewan Day in August in 2012.

Shelley preparing to deliver Goody Bags to the people at the
Bounty Reserve 2012.

Shelley with a friend at a Prince Albert fundraiser she helped organize in partnership with a local funeral home to support the sisters' swimming pool.

Shelley at a Halloween party at the Royal Canadian Legion, 2012.

The Morning I Walked Her Home

Shelley in 2012.

Shelley with a friend who was terminally ill in 2012.

The Morning I Walked Her Home

Shelley Fraser

Chapter Twenty-Eight
Rising Strong

2013 marked a pivotal year in my life, a year of healing, transformation, and self-discovery. After jaw surgery and recovering from multiple injuries, including concussions and chronic pain from car accidents, I found myself at a crossroads. Physio sessions became more than rehabilitation. They became a revelation. I began to uncover physical strength I had not realized I possessed.

At physiotherapy, I stood out. Fellow participants often commented on my endurance, while others admitted they felt worn out. My physiotherapist affectionately nicknamed me the "Cardio Queen," saying, "We have no problem getting Shelley motivated." My pain management counselor echoed the sentiment, calling me a role model.

I was not there to compete. I was there to challenge myself. Each goal I set became a steppingstone to the next. I realized my determination had always been there. I just needed to tap into it in a unique way. Despite the pain, both physical and emotional, I believed that daily challenges, even small ones, could move me forward. It was not easy. There were moments of reflection, setbacks, and times when I had to reignite my motivation. But I kept going.

After physio, I often returned to the gym. Exercise became my medicine. It helped me manage pain, prevent severe muscle spasms, and sharpen my cognitive abilities. I learned that movement does not have to be intense to be effective. Whether it was a short walk or a light workout, staying active was essential, especially as I aged.

2013 was also a turning point, a year when I felt my life needed a new direction. I had already accomplished so much, writing short stories, working, volunteering, and studying. I even helped install a bell on the Catholic church at the Bounty Reserve. But I felt the need for something different, something that would challenge me in a new way. My life was evolving, and I sensed a shift coming, one that required a different kind of courage.

The Morning I Walked Her Home

Although I still attended Bounty Church occasionally, it had become part of my past. The joy I once felt was gone. The respect I once held had faded, and I began to feel used, valued only for my ability to fundraise and generate income for the church. What I received in return was not appreciation, but resentment and anger.

I came to a painful realization that my spirituality had been fractured, not by faith itself, but by the people who ran the church. It was a quiet kind of heartbreak, the kind that does not shout but lingers. I knew I had to search for my own spiritual path, one that did not rely on attending services or being part of an institution. I discovered that true spirituality comes from within. You do not need a church to be spiritual.

Growing up around religious sisters and priests, I was never influenced by their beliefs. If anything, I saw their humanity more than their holiness. In earlier years, I enjoyed church services, the social connections, and the activities. But over time, I realized I could find those same experiences elsewhere, without the emotional toll.

As I grew stronger in body and spirit, I knew the next chapter would not be about returning to old patterns. It would be about embracing new horizons, where resilience, independence, and faith in myself would guide the way.

Shelley Fraser

Chapter Twenty-Nine
Choosing My Own Path

In 2014, I finally made the difficult but necessary decision to walk away from the Catholic Church at the Bounty Reserve. That spring, I attended my final service and gathered all my belongings. It wasn't a sudden choice; I had been thinking about it for months. The church no longer held my interest. Stepping away meant challenging myself to stay out of a place that had become unhealthy. It wasn't only about leaving; it was about reclaiming my peace.

I found purpose elsewhere, working in education and teaching English as a Second Language (ESL) to adult newcomers to Canada. It reminded me of my time teaching ESL in Africa back in 2007 with seminarians. Watching adult learners progress and eventually receive their certificates was deeply rewarding.

That spring brought sorrow. I received word that Sister Yvonne had passed away. Surprisingly, many people at the Bounty Reserve didn't hear about her death until days later. Sister Yvonne had served the community for nearly twenty years. People said, "Had we known, we would have attended her service." Even Sister Wendy was shocked, saying, "For a woman who gave so much of herself, why wasn't the community notified?" It felt as though her legacy had been quietly tucked away when it deserved to be honored openly. I attended the funeral at the "Big House" and reconnected with friends. I also learned that Sister John, who had been Sister Yvonne's companion for eight years, was now in Quebec.

Personally, things were beginning to shift in a positive way. I spoke with my former Biology teacher, a friend since 1991. She said, "It will take a long time, Shelley, to get over these sisters. They were a part of your life, especially Sister John." She was right; it would take years. That year, I continued going to the gym and challenging myself physically. I chose to embrace solitude, stepping away from the spotlight and leaning into a quieter life. In the past, my work at the

Bounty Reserve and in Hope often appeared in newspaper articles. But now, I needed time to heal both emotionally and physically. I secluded myself from certain people and surrounded myself only with those who were positive influences. It was the only way I could truly find myself.

Meanwhile, my friend Joe's health was declining, and he had moved into a nursing home. I didn't see him as often, but I cherished our time together, especially when he made sharp, funny comments about Sister John or Sister Doris. He would get irritated when they called wanting to speak to me, feeling they were taking my attention away. He was protective of me, and maybe a little jealous. Outsiders often see things we don't. Joe was humorous and deeply caring. To this day, I still laugh at some of the things he said about the sisters. Those years were exciting in their own way. I hadn't realized how much energy I had brought to those older folks, but it was fun and kept them on their toes.

In November, we learned my father had cancer. I didn't know until my brother Stewart called and said, "You're a hard person to find…" He had tried contacting me and, knowing I was once close to Sister John, reached out to her at the "Big House." To his surprise, she said, "I haven't heard from Shelley for a few years." She later called him back with a contact number for the sisters at the Bounty Reserve and added, "We will pray for your dad." My brother thanked her and eventually reached me. He said, "I'm surprised you're no longer in contact with Sister John. I thought you two were always close." I didn't go into why we had fallen out of touch.

Thanks to Sister John providing that contact number, I was able to spend time with my father during his illness, something I might have missed otherwise. In that moment, I realized that even broken connections can still offer grace.

The Morning I Walked Her Home

Chapter Thirty
Farewell to Two Important Men

On New Year's Eve 2014 and January 1st, 2015, my dad and his girlfriend Louise hosted a party at her place. Many of his friends and some of his children were there, including myself. It was a warm gathering. As the night wound down, Louise asked everyone to leave except me. She said, "Everyone must leave but Shelley can stay." I stayed overnight.

That evening, I received a surprise phone call from friends in Calgary wishing me a Happy New Year. Their thoughtfulness touched me. The next morning, Louise told me, "Sister Doris was asking about you." By then, I had already left the Bounty Reserve church and had no interest in returning.

During Dad's illness with cancer, I had some quiet moments with him. In one conversation, he said about my mom, "She always wanted to leave." He didn't elaborate, and I didn't press. Dad was a man who believed people should always be doing something. Years later, Louise told me he had been hard on his children and partners. When he entered a room, people often froze, unsure of how he'd react. But he never bothered me.

My mom used to say I had a lot of my dad's personality, especially when I got angry. I'd curse just like him. It amazed me how DNA can shape you, even when you haven't grown up around someone. Dad loved music, especially Hank Williams. He admired anyone who could play a musical instrument. My grandfather also loved music. He played the banjo, and our home was often filled with sound.

Joe passed away in early January. He had been ill for a long time. Though I was disappointed, I felt relieved his suffering had ended. Joe was someone I could confide in completely. He was trustworthy, and as Sister John once beautifully said, "Listen to Joe, he is a wise old owl." He could see things I couldn't. He was intellectual, empathetic, and generous-hearted. We shared and laughed a lot. He was my rock when I needed someone who would listen. His absence left a quiet space in my life that no one else could fill.

In February, Dad's health declined rapidly. He was hospitalized, and I visited often before work or on weekends. He was rarely alone; friends visited regularly. I once overheard him say, "I'd like to live to 70, like my dad." Sadly, he passed at 67 in the early hours of February 19, 2015.

I was grateful for the time we shared, thanks to Sister John, who helped my brother contact me. My sister later told me Dad had said, "Shelley came back. I guess she's no longer mad at me." But I was never angry. We simply never had a close relationship.

After my parents divorced, Dad built a new life with another woman and had more children. I didn't feel I had a place in that life. I learned to live without a father figure. Still, he was protective. When I had conflicts with the sisters, he'd tell my friend, "Keep her away from them." He didn't want me to hurt.

In the early 2000s, when I lived in Hope, he would check in on me. Sister John once said I looked like him and called him a good-looking man. She knew him only a little.

After Dad passed, I drove sixteen hours to Calgary and back to pick up my youngest brother, Todd, for the funeral. I cried most of the way. I thought about Dad's life. He had a hard life, losing his mother young and growing up with a father who struggled with alcoholism and grief. He had also lost his girlfriend to suicide in 1986 and raised her children as his own. Not many men would do that. It made him remarkable in ways I didn't fully appreciate until later.

His funeral was held at Elk's Hall since he wasn't Catholic. The weather was poor and snowy. My eldest brother Stewart didn't attend, but he had said goodbye at the hospital.

At the funeral, I placed a letter in Dad's casket. It was my way of finding closure. Writing those letters helped me say what I couldn't always speak aloud. It was my final gift. I had done the same for my mom, Aunt Jenny, and Sister John. I also read Psalm 23 aloud. It was a beautiful service. Dad had many friends. His two sisters and their children came, as did my other siblings. I thanked everyone for coming despite the weather and expressed my gratitude to my siblings.

After the funeral, I went straight back to work. My boss was surprised and said, "You don't need to be here." I replied, "I need to stay busy." That's how I cope with grief, by keeping myself moving.

While preparing for Dad's estate auction, one day a man and his wife showed up. I told Louise I didn't care much for him. She replied, "Your dad felt the same way." That surprised me. Dad had strong opinions.

That year, I kept myself busy. We held Dad's estate sale in May, and in July I had shoulder surgery. I continued working with adult learners and felt content. I was adjusting and finding my own way.

Despite the losses that year, I didn't reach out to Sister John as I had after my mom's death. That part of me stayed quiet. I kept to myself and visited others. Losing Joe and Dad just weeks apart was heavy. They were two men I deeply admired. Their loss marked the end of an era in my life. But in their memory, I found the strength to keep going.

The Morning I Walked Her Home

Shelley Fraser

Chapter Thirty-One
Healing and the Counselling Journey

In 2016, while continuing my work in education, I felt a deeper calling to explore mental health. That year, I began studying counselling, focusing on areas such as addictions, child abuse, domestic violence, and trauma. I also took courses in Pastoral Care in the United States while continuing to work with newcomers to Canada. These studies were not just academic; they were part of my own healing. I was searching for answers to unresolved parts of my life.

I completed my counselling program with highest honors. I believe that understanding others begins with understanding ourselves, and that is not always easy. It requires empathy, introspection, and the willingness to listen. Everyone has a story, and every story deserves to be heard and valued.

Personal growth often involves rewiring our thinking. We must evaluate our experiences and recognize what is working and what is not. If something no longer serves us, change becomes necessary. Transformation is ongoing, and this applies to relationships as well. Many expect relationships to remain the same, but without evolution they become stagnant. Growth requires space, and healthy relationships allow room for each person to develop.

Communication is vital. I often tell my students to check in with their children daily. It does not require hours. Even a simple question such as "How was your day?" can build connection. This was missing in my own youth. My mother worked during the week, and I only saw her on weekends. My parents were not emotionally present, and my grandfather was distant, weighed down by his own unresolved grief.

The power of mentorship can change a life. Thankfully, I had someone who cared. Sister John was my lifeline during my formative years and helped shape who I am today. The transition from youth to adulthood was not always smooth. Boundaries were tested often, but as my brother Stewart once said, "Sister John shook the boundaries but never pushed them over." That kind of love and commitment leaves a lasting imprint.

I remind my students that if they see a youth struggling, they should take the time to ask how they are doing. That simple act of kindness can change a life. We all leave marks on others, so it is important to be patient and kind. Many people are broken and do not even know it, but they do not have to stay that way. There is always hope for a better tomorrow.

Rediscovering self-worth must come from within, not from others. Seeking external validation can make us lose sight of who we are. Depression often stems from the loss of self. While many experience it, it is important not to remain in that space for too long. Support is essential, and seeking help is a sign of strength, not weakness.

I often compare support to being stuck in snow or mud. When someone stops to help you get your car unstuck, the relief is overwhelming. That is what support feels like. Help is available, but it must be welcomed, not forced.

The same is true for those who struggle with addiction and pain. Addiction is often rooted in pain. Many who struggle do not understand why, but they are still worthy individuals with gifts to offer. I have faced my own struggles. For years, I masked my pain with alcohol and pushed loved ones away, believing I was not deserving of love. Beneath that pain was a giving and loving person. I have long since stopped using alcohol to cope because I now understand the reasons behind my behavior. Recognition is the first step toward change. It took time, but I began to see myself clearly, not as broken, but as becoming.

Change takes time and effort. There is no magic wand. Life is not easy, and it was never meant to be. We are all unique, facing different challenges, and that is what makes life interesting. Imagine a world where everyone faced the same problems. It would be dull.

Living in the present has become my practice. Each morning, I welcome a new day and new challenges. Every day is different, and it is important to stay present. We cannot change the past, but we can learn from it, grow, and do better. Living in the past hinders our present. The world keeps moving with or without us.

Since completing my education, practicum, and earning my certification as a professional counsellor, life has become more enriching. I am more mindful of others' behaviors, including my own. The world is not perfect, but it is manageable. I am grateful for the skills I have gained in counselling and education, two passions I deeply enjoy.

Through counselling and service, I discovered that healing is not only about mending the past but about transforming pain into purpose. It is a path that continues to shape the next chapter of my journey.

On March 28, 2016, I was driving on 15th Street West in Prince Albert when I noticed Sister John walking in front of the "Big House." She looked lost in thought, as if meditating. I did not stop, but I carried that image with me. Later, I learned her sister had passed away that same day. Somehow, it made sense. Grief and grace often walk together. I remember that day vividly because it was my birthday.

The Morning I Walked Her Home

Shelley Fraser

Chapter Thirty-Two
A Year of Recognition and Resilience

The year 2017 was a busy one for me. I continued my work with newcomers to Canada and maintained my status as a licensed professional counsellor. I also dedicated my time to the Royal Canadian Legion during poppy season, a tradition I had supported for many years. I had always volunteered wholeheartedly, never expecting anything in return.

Then, to my surprise, I received a phone call from the Premier's Office in Regina. I was informed that I was one of ten recipients of the Saskatchewan Volunteer Medal for outstanding volunteerism in 2016. I was thrilled. My brother Stewart called to congratulate me and asked how I felt. Honestly, I did not feel much different, although it was a wonderful honor. Stewart said, "You have put Hope on the map." I was the only person from my community to ever receive this award.

Recognition has always humbled me. I understood the effort behind every achievement. I was a woman of action, never one to sit on the sidelines. Words meant little if the work was not done. Taking action was what mattered.

When it was time to gather in Regina, a friend from Calgary joined me for the ceremonies. We had photos taken of the Premier of Saskatchewan and a group photo with all the recipients. Each of us received a large certificate and a volunteer medal. During lunch, one of the MLAs sat with us and visited. I spoke with several others as well. I believe I was the youngest recipient that year.

If Sister John had known about this, I am sure she would have been proud. She was living at the "Big House" at the time. My achievements were part of the legacy she helped shape. It had been nearly six years since I last had contact with her. Over time, I found myself thinking about her less. I was building a life of my own, and for the first time in years, things felt calm. I was content. I finally felt like I was living for myself.

The Morning I Walked Her Home

Both of my parents had passed and so had Joe. It made the celebration a quiet one, but meaningful all the same. On my way back through Saskatoon, I met my brother and his wife. They wanted to see the award, so I showed them. Stewart said, "You should be proud of that." I was, but I stayed humble. I repeated something Sister John had once told me, "That is another feather you can stick in your hat."

That summer, I underwent shoulder surgery. My shoulders had endured a lot of abuse over the years. It is no different from people who struggle with knee or joint issues. Then in November, I was rear ended in Calgary and sustained neck, back, shoulder, and jaw injuries. I later needed jaw surgery to repair the damage. Since then, I have had two more shoulder surgeries and dealt with blood clot issues in my left leg.

Although the year held many good moments, my health took a hit. Still, I had unbelievable determination and refused to let injuries define my well-being. I believed that once you let physical limitations take over, you might as well admit defeat. I had a life to live, and I was not going to let pain stop me.

I knew what it would take to feel like myself again. I had done it before. It would require physical therapy, massage therapy, proper pain management counselling, and, most importantly, believing I could recover and keep going.

As I think about all the accidents and surgeries I have endured, I'm struck by how my outlook remains surprisingly optimistic. I am grateful that I am a survivor. I have been through so much, but I live each day with gratitude and faith, knowing my journey still has meaning. Not every day is perfect or pain free. I suffer from chronic pain quite often, but I choose not to focus on it. At this stage of life, I want to live fully. That belief is my anchor. It steadies me when the pain flares or when memories surface.

A cousin of Sister John's once said, "If God does not want us yet, it is because we still have work to do." I believe that. There are still lessons to learn and people to meet. We were all put on this earth for a reason. When we were born, we had no idea where life would lead us.

Had I known my parents would divorce, that I would suffer multiple injuries and abuse, or that a religious sister would take me under her wing instead of my own parents, I might have said, "The heck with this," and preferred not to be born. But God, or the Creator if you prefer, has a purpose for each of us. In a way, our map was drawn before we arrived. We simply do not know what life is going to throw our way. And as someone once said, it is a good thing we don't, or we would spend our days worrying about a life we have no control over.

This is where philosophy gently enters our lives. We search for meaning in the chaos and wonder why things unfold the way they do. But perhaps the deeper truth is that we are not meant to know everything. Life unfolds in mystery, and our role is to respond with courage, compassion, and purpose. We are not just passengers. We are active participants in a story still being written.

Life is short, and as we age, it seems to move even faster. I reflect on the many losses I have endured, beginning with my baby sister. I carried grief from a young age. I learned that people eventually leave us, but we are never fully prepared, even when we know it is coming.

It is important to remember that when you leave this world, do not leave with regrets. Life is short enough. Appreciate each day and live as though it might be your last, because you never truly know. Everyone will experience both loss and success. Your sense of success will come from how you reflect on your life. Challenge yourself, only yourself, and you will discover that life can offer both happiness and fulfillment. Because in the end, it is not about how others see you. It is about how you see yourself.

True resilience is not the absence of pain. It is the courage to keep living with gratitude and purpose.

In 2017, Shelley received the Saskatchewan Volunteer Medal for her outstanding volunteer service and community involvement.

Shelley Fraser

Chapter Thirty-Three
Echoes of Legends

In 2018, I took a cross-country tour of the United States, a journey I had made several times before, yet each trip always offered something new. I carefully planned my route, driving through multiple states to visit places filled with history and personal meaning.

My journey began in Texas. In Dallas, I visited the site of President John F. Kennedy's 1963 assassination. Touring the Sixth Floor Museum at Dealey Plaza, once the Texas School Book Depository, I sat quietly, reflecting on the gravity of that moment as if I had been there myself. The silence in that space was haunting.

From there, I headed northeast to Arkansas, where I explored the William J. Clinton Presidential Library in Little Rock. The exhibits brought history to life, from the challenges of his presidency to personal artifacts, including information about Monica Lewinsky and a letter from John F. Kennedy Jr.

Next, I traveled to Missouri, stopping in Mansfield to visit the home of Laura Ingalls Wilder. Walking through the house where she lived and wrote her beloved books felt quietly meaningful.

Passing through St. Louis, I paused to admire the Gateway Arch, a towering symbol of westward expansion that seemed to touch the sky.

Continuing east, I entered Tennessee. In Memphis, I toured Graceland, Elvis Presley's home. It was smaller than I had imagined from television and very commercialized, yet still touching to stand in the place he once called home. Elvis's music played softly, souvenir displays lined the halls, and even the hamburgers at the on-site restaurant carried a sense of nostalgia.

In Nashville, I visited the Country Music Hall of Fame and the Ernest Tubb Record Shop.

From there, I drove to Camden, where Patsy Cline's plane crashed in 1963. At the memorial park, I left a rose and a note in her memory, sitting quietly in reflection.

I also visited Loretta Lynn's Ranch, where I saw the bus and jeep featured in Coal Miner's Daughter. It was a humble but heartfelt tribute to her strength and enduring career.

From Tennessee, I headed north to Iowa, where I visited the crash site near Clear Lake where Buddy Holly, Ritchie Valens, and the Big Bopper died in 1959. The memorial, nearly a mile into a field, was marked with plaques and their hit records. Standing there in silence, I thought about how young they were and how much they had already given to the world.

In Illinois, I stopped in Springfield to visit President Abraham Lincoln's tomb at Oak Ridge Cemetery. A local woman told me that President Kennedy had visited during his campaign in the early 1960s, a detail that felt both fascinating and strangely comforting.

Driving south to Alabama, I visited the Hank Williams Museum. His music, filled with heartache and truth, had always resonated with me. At the cemetery where he and his wife are buried, I stood quietly, letting the lyrics of his songs echo in my mind.

Heading northeast, I entered Virginia. In Winchester, Patsy Cline's hometown, I toured her house and learned that her mother had delivered her just nine days after her own birthday, a coincidence that mirrored my own birth story. I purchased a commemorative brick from her home and visited her gravesite, reflecting on her legacy.

In Schuyler, I visited the real-life home of Earl Hamner Jr., the inspiration behind The Waltons. The house differed slightly from the television version but carried the same warmth.

Virginia's rolling hills and quiet roads offered timeless beauty.

From there, I drove into Washington, D.C., a city alive with government officials and relentless traffic. I passed federal buildings before crossing into Arlington, Virginia, to pay respects at the graves

The Morning I Walked Her Home

of President John F. Kennedy, Jackie Kennedy, and Senator Robert Kennedy. I left roses at each site and took photos. Arlington National Cemetery is a place of deep reverence, its history undeniable. Overlooking it stands Arlington House, the Robert E. Lee Memorial, commanding a view of the capital city.

Continuing northeast, I passed through Baltimore and Philadelphia before reaching New York City. Heavy traffic kept me in the city for over four hours. At one point, an ambulance approached from behind, and I had to maneuver carefully to let it pass. I stayed calm, and thankfully, everything worked out.

My final destinations were in Massachusetts. In Boston, I visited the John F. Kennedy Presidential Library, then drove to Hyannis Port on Cape Cod, the Kennedy family's summer home. Cape Cod has always been a place where I feel at peace by the ocean.

Ironically, in July 1999, John F. Kennedy Jr.'s plane went down near that area. I did not realize he was missing until I returned to Arlington and saw his parents' gravesite surrounded by flowers. Like the rest of the world, I was shocked and hopeful, but sadly, he had passed.

Years later, I learned that Sister John had been nearby visiting her sister at Cape Cod at the same time. We were only hours apart.

Throughout this journey, I honored many icons who gave so much to the world, even though their lives were cut short. The trip became a quiet reflection on how precious life is and how quickly it can be taken. Each stop reminded me that behind every monument lies a story of love, loss, and resilience.

One thing I can say about the United States is that it holds tightly to its history. You can feel it in the old buildings, the music, and the memorials. Though I was not alive during many of these losses, they still affect me, as if grief and hope can travel through time.

Whether listening to Hank Williams' sorrowful ballads, Patsy Cline's "Sweet Dreams," Elvis Presley's "It's Over," Buddy Holly's "Rave On," Ritchie Valens' "La Bamba," or the Big Bopper's "Chantilly Lace," their voices still echo. These artists had dreams and gave back to their country. Their paths were often scrutinized, but they never gave up.

In life, wherever you go, you will meet naysayers, people who are jealous, who do not understand, or who lack passion. But those who persevere, who believe in their purpose, leave behind legacies that echo through time. Travel became my way of connecting with the past, honoring legacy, and finding healing through remembrance. It was a tribute to the enduring influence of American icons and the places that preserve their stories.

As 2018 wound down, I texted my brother on December 8 saying, "Sister John will be turning 80 today." Instinctively, I added, "She will more than likely survive another five years." I was nearly accurate. She passed eight days after her 86th birthday.

By then it had been over seven years since I last spoke to her. Time had created distance.

Some legacies do not fade. They echo quietly like a familiar song.

Through remembrance and travel, I found healing in the legacies of those whose voices still echo.

The Morning I Walked Her Home

Shelley Fraser

Chapter Thirty-Four
Teaching Roots, Counselling Wings

In 2019, I continued to struggle with ongoing shoulder issues, which eventually led me to make a career change. Sometimes change is painful but necessary, and sometimes it quietly brings good. With a background in counselling, I decided to explore the idea of starting private practice. To do that, I needed a business plan, which included assessing whether Prince Albert would be a suitable location. Part of this process involved collecting at least thirty community questionnaires, and I exceeded that goal by gathering over one hundred.

Starting a business also meant doing extensive research. Honestly, I wasn't sure I could get it off the ground, but my intuition told me otherwise. I was torn between continuing to teach and pursuing counselling. Even in the classroom, I often found myself listening, guiding, and helping students navigate challenges beyond language. Counselling simply gave me a new way to offer the same kind of care. At the same time, I focused on healing through physiotherapy and massage treatments. Recovery takes time, and we often want to rush it, but the mind and body do not always move at the same pace.

It was heartbreaking to say goodbye to teaching ESL to newcomers to Canada. Over the years, I learned that when you let go of something, there is always something to gain, even if you cannot yet see what that will be. When I told my students I would no longer be teaching, they wrote a letter asking the staff to keep me and even offered to help with my tasks. It was incredibly thoughtful, but I knew it was not possible. Their kindness stayed with me and reminded me that teaching is not just about lessons. It is about relationships.

The students organized a farewell meal, gave me a gift card and a card, and my organization took us all out for snacks and bowling. At the time, I had a large class. I met the new instructor and introduced her to the students. She was younger and had never taught adult learners before.

Teaching adult learners is unique. Many bring a wealth of life experience and are eager to learn, working hard to achieve their goals. These newcomers to Canada had sacrificed a great deal for a better life for themselves and their families. My role was to help them speak, understand, read, and write English. Like learning any new language, it takes time and practice. If you don't use it, you lose it.

I taught students from China, Japan, the Philippines, India, Russia, Vietnam, Africa, Ukraine, Korea, and more. It was a rewarding experience. Many struggled with adapting to Canadian culture, and I had to develop empathy for their journey. I understood their challenges. I had experienced something similar when I was in Uganda.

Some students stood out. One woman from Congo spoke only French when she joined the program. She failed her first Canadian Citizenship exam by just a few marks and used to avoid English speakers. After completing our program, she passed her second exam, became a Canadian citizen, and now works at a local hospital. She owns a home, drives her own vehicle, and supports herself and her son with pride. We still keep in touch.

Another student from China once said, "How Shelley teaches is how they teach us in China. The teacher provides instruction, assigns the work, we finish it and hand it in for marking." A student from Japan now lives in Kelowna with her husband and two children and still reaches out occasionally.

All students entering our program had to take an entrance exam to determine their suitability. In all my years teaching ESL, I only had to turn one student away. Her skills were not yet at the level needed for the program, and I did not want her to struggle. She was upset at first but later thanked me by email for referring her to another agency.

Weeks later, I ran into a former student at Burger King. He said, "Shelley, I am the only remaining student in the class." I asked what had happened, and he explained that everyone had quit. The instructor had stayed for a while but eventually left. A year later, another instructor took over, but sadly, I later learned she had taken her life.

In education, consistency is crucial. Students adapt to an instructor's style, and changing teachers' mid-year can be disruptive. Eventually, they found a consistent instructor, which was a relief.

It is remarkable how someone's presence can leave a lasting mark. When I stepped down as Ladies Auxiliary president in 2007, the role remained unfilled for some time. The same happened when I left the Bounty Reserve church; the fundraising simply changed. And again, when I left my ESL teaching role, it took a while before someone else could take it on. Sometimes you don't realize the depth of your impact until you step away. And even then, it echoes.

The truth is no one does it alone. Success requires a team, but it also depends on a strong leader who is willing to commit and see things through. Leadership is not about being perfect. It is about showing up, staying dedicated, and leaving behind something that matters.

Teaching planted the roots of connection, while counselling gave me wings to help others heal.

The Morning I Walked Her Home

Shelley Fraser

Chapter Thirty-Five
Living Through the Covid-19 Pandemic

In 2020, the world was thrown into chaos as a mysterious virus spread rapidly, causing illness and, tragically, taking lives. Governments around the globe responded with lockdowns and strict health measures. Social interaction became limited, and many found themselves in isolation. Visiting friends and family was no longer safe or allowed, especially in hospitals and nursing homes, which created immense emotional strain.

Masks became mandatory in public spaces, an inconvenience for many. Over time, skepticism grew as people questioned the severity of the pandemic and the rapid development of vaccines. In many workplaces, vaccination became a requirement to keep one's job, and proof of vaccination was often necessary to enter restaurants or public venues. Concerns circulated about how quickly the vaccines had been developed and whether they would work for everyone.

During this period, I was seriously considering opening a private counselling practice, but the world felt too uncertain to take on that kind of financial risk. At home, I was caring for an elderly woman who lived with me, and the weight of that responsibility shaped every decision I made. Not long after, I developed a blood clot in my leg and was hospitalized, which meant I would be on lifelong blood thinners. At the same time, stories and rumors were spreading about strokes, heart attacks, cancers, and even claims of infertility linked to the vaccines. The mix of fear, misinformation, and genuine confusion created an atmosphere that was difficult to navigate.

The world had shifted dramatically, and isolation became the new norm. Students lost the chance to interact in classrooms, and office workers transitioned to remote work. The pandemic significantly affected people's overall well-being, especially their mental health.

Even after restrictions were lifted, many remained fearful of social contact, with some refusing to leave their homes out of fear of contracting COVID. It was a dark time for many, as human connection is vital for mental and emotional health.

Fortunately, technology became a lifeline, allowing people to stay connected through cell phones and computers, even if only virtually. However, for those unfamiliar with digital tools, the experience was isolating and frustrating.

Today, we live in a world shaped by the pandemic. Mental health issues have surged, even with improvements in support systems. Many still carry scars from that time. The COVID pandemic was more than a health crisis. It was a profound disruption to how we live, connect, and care for one another.

Shelley Fraser

Chapter Thirty-Six
Teaching and Mental Health

In 2021, after a period away from teaching, I made the decision to return. I missed the interaction and the joy of watching students grow. For a while, I wasn't sure which path to follow, the classroom or counselling. I even considered pursuing a master's degree in education, but before committing, I wanted to make sure the passion was still there. So, I waited. And yes, the passion remained.

Upon returning to work, I started as a Teaching Assistant, tutoring at a college. I had an office, but the days felt long, and few students needed assistance. I felt I could do more in a classroom setting. Eventually, my supervisors assigned me to fill in for other teachers, which I didn't mind. Shortly after, an instructor left her position, and I was asked to step in. The moment I entered the classroom; I knew that was where I belonged. My passion was in teaching, and I needed to stay there.

Later, I transitioned into a new role teaching mental health and wellness at the post-secondary level. It was a perfect fit, blending my counselling background with my teaching skills. During that time, I also worked as a teacher's assistant at a university, working closely with a professor who asked me to continue with her. I accepted. Education felt like goal-setting, helping students move toward success.

In 2022, I began teaching post-secondary mental health and wellness to Indigenous students. I worked alongside other instructors to prepare them for careers in the field. Many students arrived with unresolved traumas, which could be overwhelming. Some carried layers of issues that could not be addressed in a classroom. Still, I found joy in supporting those who were eager to make a difference.

Some students believed the program itself would fix their problems, but many needed more personalized counselling. Others struggled with addictions and ongoing mental health concerns. It's important to treat people with respect and empathy, but healing requires effort. People must look inward and evaluate the changes they need to make.

Unfortunately, many fear change and cling to familiar patterns. Transformation is gradual, often unnoticed until a crisis forces it.

In 2023, I continued teaching in post-secondary mental health studies and decided to pursue my master's degree in education. I began working with a new group of students. Most were enthusiastic about learning, but some resisted change and disliked structure, which was reflected in their behavior. Some were grounded, while others frequently complained about expectations.

I often reminded them, "In the real world, you wouldn't get away with that." One student expressed a desire to be friends with their clients during therapy. I advised, "You need to maintain professional boundaries." Some lacked the maturity required for the field, though perhaps they would develop it over time.

Structure was a challenge for many, especially those from homes with little or none at all. In mental health work, one must be organized, meet deadlines, and be prepared to advocate effectively. Advocates must also do their own healing, share their stories, and understand that what worked for them may not work for others. Helpers should never dictate how someone should live. A client must determine what's best for them. Giving unsolicited advice can do more harm than good.

One day, I had a meaningful encounter with two students, a mother named Emily and her daughter, Kaylee. We shared experiences, and they were both thoughtful and eager to learn. During our conversation, Emily mentioned "the sisters." I noticed her cross necklace and assumed she might be Catholic.

I asked, "Which sisters?" She referred to the order and mentioned she had worked for them for many years as a care aide. I asked if she knew Sister John. She confirmed and expressed frustration. "Oh, Sister John would get mad and accuse me of taking her walking stick, when I didn't..." She described her as a difficult person.

I responded, "I haven't seen Sister John in many years and have no intention of doing so." Too much time had passed, and I didn't want to reopen old wounds. I had worked hard to rediscover myself and didn't want to regress. At this point, I rarely thought about her, and I wanted to keep it that way. I genuinely believed I would never cross paths with Sister John again after twelve or thirteen years of separation.

Shelley Fraser

Chapter Thirty-Seven
A Letter to Sister John

In early 2024, Emily sat near my desk in class. We exchanged small talk about her past, about mine, and sometimes about Sister John. As the weeks passed, my feelings began to shift, and I started to reconsider the idea of seeing Sister John again. Emily mentioned that she was now living in a care home facility, and I held on to that detail. I thought about it for months.

That summer, as I prepared for shoulder surgery, I found myself reflecting during recovery. One afternoon in the kitchen, I wondered how I could even approach seeing Sister John after so many years. I had no idea if she would remember me, or how clear her memory would be. I asked Emily, "Do you think it would be better if I write her a letter first and send some photos?" I also asked if she would mind delivering it.

When I began writing, emotions surfaced. I had buried many of our shared experiences. The letter was deeply personal, and I didn't want anyone else to read it. It carried pieces of our history. Without revealing too much, I mentioned moments from my youth, like when she met me at the bus during a town blackout. I wrote, "Even though people grow older, a person can still have the same heart." I added, "I know time is not on our side," and shared what I was currently doing.

Giving the letter to Emily felt like a way to gauge whether it was worth visiting. If Sister John didn't recognize my name or who I was, I would have to let it go. But Emily kept putting off delivering it. When I asked, "Did you take the letter and photos to Sister John yet?" she admitted she hadn't. I sensed she was reluctant because of how Sister John had treated her in the past.

Eventually, I said to Emily, "I think I should take this letter myself." Time was ticking, and I didn't know how much longer Sister John had. Emily met me at school with the letter, the photos, and a small gift bag. I asked, "What's in it?" She said, "Sister John likes Pepsi and Kit Kat bars." I replied, "Okay. I'll be sure to give this to her when I see her. Thank you."

That day, I reviewed my letter again, added more details, and included my phone number. I also wrote that I would return to see her the following month, in August. I wanted to give both of us time to process our thoughts and emotions. I didn't want to just show up unannounced.

July 21 was a beautiful day. The sun was out, and I was extremely nervous. It had been years since I'd last seen Sister John, and I didn't know what to expect. Before heading to the care home, I bought more Pepsi and Kit Kat bars to make sure she had enough.

When I arrived, I parked in front of a memorial bench where three women were sitting. I got out and began chatting with them. They were friendly and said they were visiting a relative in the care home. The longer we talked, the more nervous I felt, and one of the ladies kindly offered to deliver my big brown envelope with the letter, photos, and treats to Sister John.

While she went inside, I nervously continued talking with the other two women. One of them even knew one of my students. I waited anxiously for the lady to return. When she did, I asked how it went. She said, "The sister knows who you are." I was stunned. "Really?" I asked. She replied, "Yes, she said you were her favorite student and that you used to follow her around." I smiled and admitted, "I did visit her when she moved to different places."

The lady had taken a brief video and showed me Sister John receiving the envelope and treats. She said, "Sister John wants to see you." I hesitated. "Now?" I asked. "Yes," she said. I replied, "I'm not ready yet." One of the women asked why. I explained, "I haven't seen her in twelve or thirteen years." I reminded them that I had written in the letter that I would come back next month, in August. One of the women cautioned, "She may not be here next month." I smiled and said, "She will be here."

The Morning I Walked Her Home

I visited with the women a bit longer, thanked the lady who delivered the envelope and treats, and said, "I'd better get out of here before she comes looking for me."

As I got into my car, I felt a rush of excitement that Sister John remembered me. Now I had to prepare to see her. That entire month, I was restless, plagued by sleepless nights and contemplation. Had I made the right decision to revisit this after more than a decade?

But when I wrote to Sister John and told her I would come and see her the following month, I knew I had to follow through. Over the years, I had learned that one of my strengths was sticking with my decisions. I also realized how much had changed since I last saw her. I had grown personally during our time apart. Did I really want to revisit that?

Some doors, once closed, are easily left untouched. But others call us quietly, until we answer.

I had to acknowledge that Sister John was very much a part of who I became. Our connection was about healing, closure, and the courage to revisit meaningful relationships from the past.

Sometimes closure begins with a letter, opening the door to memory and healing.

Sister John marked Shelley's envelope with four stars, a tender, unpredictable detail that mirrored the four months they shared before her passing.

The Morning I Walked Her Home

Shelley Fraser

Chapter Thirty-Eight
A Reunion Meant to Happen

On August 16, the long-awaited day to reunite with Sister John finally arrived. I invited Emily and another student, Shayna, to join me. Emily already knew Sister John, but Shayna did not. The day before, I called the care home to let them know I would be visiting. I told the students I would bring pop, water, and cheesecake, and I picked up a bouquet of flowers, something I had sent her before, knowing she would appreciate it.

I must admit, I was nervous. The suspense had been building for nearly a month. When the three of us arrived at the care home, we walked through the doors and were greeted by a Catholic priest sitting near the entrance, who said hello. The place felt smaller than I had imagined. As we rode the elevator up, my heart raced. My mind was full, and I wasn't sure what to expect or how I would feel.

It was around 2:45 on a beautiful Friday afternoon when we approached Sister John's room. I let Emily step inside first, then I followed. Shayna, who had also worked in a care home, was equally capable, so I felt supported. Sister John was lying down resting with her eyes closed. Immediately, I noticed my large brown envelope on the corner of her end table, resting beside her as though my presence had been sitting with her even when I wasn't physically there. Seeing it there, waiting in its place, made it feel as if a part of me had already arrived before I did. In that instant, I felt the weight of all the years between us settle gently on my shoulders.

Emily gently said, "Sister… Sister, Shelley is here to see you." Sister John woke, looked at us, and said, "I didn't sleep much last night." She sat up and added, "I just recently began using my rosary." Then she asked me, "Where have you been?" I smiled and replied, "I've been around. Not far." It must have felt like a bit of a miracle to her to see me standing there again, after all those years.

The Morning I Walked Her Home

I had planned to sit near the wall by her family photos, but Emily encouraged me to take the reclining chair so I could sit closer to Sister John, and I did. As I settled in, I noticed changes in her. She no longer wore the cross around her neck, though her wedding band remained. A cross hung on her wall, but there was no religious literature on her tray or table. Family photos were visible, and a walker stood nearby. She was still herself, yet different. Her voice was familiar, though she rarely wore her glasses now.

During the visit, my thoughts shifted between past and present. At times, she felt like a stranger, yet her voice anchored me. Emily asked, "Do you remember me, Sister?" She replied, "You look familiar." I introduced her to my students, and she asked them, "Is Shelley a good teacher?" They responded, "Shelley is an awesome instructor."

Sister John spoke about her time in Rome, her voice carrying that soft mixture of memory and distance that comes with age. The students asked whether I had met her back then, and I told them no. She paused, remembering two students who had visited her there, and mentioned spending time with another sister from the U.S. Then she looked at me with a familiar spark and joked, "Did you think I don't know how to read?"

I laughed, surprised by her quickness. "Well, I didn't know what your cognitive state was like," I teased. She gave me a look of quiet amusement before asking softly, "How did you find me? And when was the last time you saw me?"

I told her the last time we met was in Saskatoon. I explained that Emily, my student, had been the one to tell me where she was. It felt as though Emily had been placed in my life for a reason. She had guided me back to someone who mattered to me, someone I once thought I might never see again.

The whole encounter felt like a small grace, a gentle reminder that people return to us in ways we don't expect, and sometimes the world arranges itself quietly to make that possible.

I asked if she still drove; she said no. I offered cheesecake, but she wasn't hungry. I opened a can of Pepsi for her, her favorite. The students then asked her about me. Sitting upright, she mentioned there had been some challenges and that I had stayed with them a few times. She was right, though we didn't elaborate.

Later, a former student of Sister John's who volunteered at the care home came in and joined us. She was older and said Sister John had taught her at school, years before I had known her. She mentioned that Sister John had kept all their artwork. Sister John turned to me. "You did art too," she said. I replied, "I wasn't really an artist; I was more into writing." It touched me that she had preserved her students' creations. We also spoke about Sister Yvonne, whom she said, "always balanced the books to a tee."

The volunteer asked if Sister John wanted to attend church, but she didn't respond. She smiled and said, 'You probably want to visit with your company.' We would have gladly left if she had wanted to attend church.

As our conversation continued, I told Sister John, "I wanted my students to know you were the one who made a difference in my life." She raised her arm and said, "Yippy." We all laughed. I made another comment, and she said "Yippy" again, lifting her arm with the same spark. I think she needed to feel validated, to see how important she had been.

As the visit was nearing the end, we signed a card for her. I said, "You were amazing." The card included a photo of her from the 1980–1981 yearbook.

We each hugged Sister John as we left. She said, "Come back anytime," and I promised I would. I told her Shayna and I were going out for supper, and she said, "That's good." She remained sitting up as we left, and I sensed she had more to say.

Before leaving, I realized I had forgotten something for her. She asked, "What are you looking for?" I said, "I had something I wanted to give you." It was fudge. I thought I had it with me, but I didn't. As I walked away, I felt numb. I wasn't sure what to make of the visit. I had changed over the years and so had she. My perceptions had shifted. Yet something about Sister John and our connection still resonated deeply, even if I couldn't fully understand it.

Afterward, I returned to school and noticed I had left the fudge on the counter. I called the care home and asked the staff, "Can you please let Sister John know I'll come back later this week? I forgot something I wanted to give her."

During the call, the care worker told me that Sister John had been excited about our visit and had been talking about it to the staff.

A reunion is not about returning to the past but finding healing in the echoes of connection.

Shelley Fraser

Chapter Thirty-Nine
Private Moments

Before I begin this chapter, I want to acknowledge that some of the intimate moments Sister John and I shared are deeply personal. Out of respect for her, I will not reveal them. What I will share are the experiences that stood out, moments that were humorous, touching, and meaningful.

When I began visiting Sister John, I often brought her favorite treats such as Pepsi and chocolate bars. Sometimes she sat up in bed, and other times she lay on the bed. Those first visits felt surreal. We were reconnecting after years apart. She was fragile, yet always happy to see me.

She often spoke about her family and shared memories from her younger years. She once said, "You remind me of my oldest sister, who had determination." I learned things I had never known. She had led a choir, gone to a movie alone, painted a car, and had a sister help her get her driver's license.

She shared some stories from her teaching years and recalled the subjects she taught. She talked about the bats in the attic at the Hope Convent and an experience from university.

On one wall, she kept a photo of her parents. She said, "There is a picture of your flowers." I was not sure whether she meant the actual flowers I had given her, but it touched me that she placed me in that same space beside her parents.

As she spoke about her mother, I said, "It sounds like she was a lovely lady. I wish I could have met her." She told me about her father playing an instrument, and I replied, "That would have been amazing." She shared how devastated she was when she lost him and how she could not attend her mother's funeral. Her heartbreak was unmistakable.

Then she added, "You lost a family member too." I nodded. "Yes, I did." We talked about attachment, and I said, "The deeper the attachment, the more it will hurt."

We also talked about risks. I said, "Sometimes in life a person needs to take risks to know who they are." Sister John was independent. She always did what she felt was right for herself. I admired that.

Her stories reminded me that she was human, not only a Catholic sister but a woman who loved, cared, and sometimes bent the rules out of respect for what she believed was right. She admitted she struggled with obedience, which did not surprise me. It was part of her nature.

She asked about my brothers. "How are the boys?" She had taught them years ago. Then she asked what I was teaching. "Mental health," I replied.

I listened to her the way she had once listened to me when I was young. The roles had reversed. I was now the supporter, and she was the one seeking support. She asked if I went to church. "No, I don't," I said. She replied, "That's okay."

As our visits became more consistent, I began bringing lunch, and we ate together. Sometimes I called the care home to ask what she liked. "Pizza," they said. So, I brought pizza. Other times I brought burgers or ice cream.

I always made sure she had enough Pepsi and chocolate bars. One day, as I unpacked the treats, she said, "Put them in the drawers so the staff doesn't see them." Then she joked, "People are going to get jealous because you are spoiling me, but I don't mind."

During one lunch, after we finished eating, she remarked that she had probably gained another pound or two. Then she complimented me on my hair and my T-shirt. In that moment, I realized she had been watching me closely. I thanked her, and she said, "Your parents would be proud of you."

The Morning I Walked Her Home

I brought photos of my family one day. She looked at my mom's obituary card and said, "I did a reading at your mom's funeral." I said, "You sure did." Her name was on the card. After looking through the photos, she said, "You have a nice-looking family."

A woman in a wheelchair came by asking for help with her wool, which had become tangled in her wheel. "I am making a toque for my grandson," she said. I helped her, and Sister John watched from the corner of her eye. When the woman left, Sister John said, "Someone else can help her." I thought, "Alright."

I often brought old yearbooks to show her. One day, I opened the 1980–1981 edition. She found her photo, then turned the page and said, "There you are." She recognized me instantly. More than forty years had passed, yet she remembered the image.

Before I left that day, I hugged her, took her hand, and helped her toward her walker. She said, "I don't know when I will see you next." I reassured her, "Don't worry, I will be back." She said, "Okay," and walked me to the elevator.

Another time, I commented on a photo of her younger self. "You were a beautiful woman," I said. She lit up with joy and teased me.

One day, as I walked in, she said, "I've been rolling this around in my mind. Even though we're not blood related, you're the one." Her words surprised me, but I believed her.

During lunch, she once said, "I don't know how I am going to repay you." I replied, "Sister, don't worry. You have given me so much." What she gave me was not material. It was love and care, and no amount of money could ever buy that.

She said, "I wasn't expecting this to happen," and then added, "I wish I had kept your things." Her words surprised me, but they touched me deeply. I realized she likely thought she would never see me again, and whatever she had kept of mine must have felt like a connection she never expected to need later in life.

The material things did not matter to me. What mattered was what we carried in our hearts.

Later, she asked, "What will your next project be?"

She often teased me, saying, "I was almost missing you," or "I was expecting you to come sooner." I would smile.

One day before I left, she asked for help zipping up her vest. The zipper was small, but I managed. She brushed her hair and smiled as I teased her. The more time I spent with her, the more my buried feelings resurfaced. I felt protective toward her, and I didn't want to see her suffer.

She asked what I thought of her room, and I said, "It's very nice. Lots of space." Then she asked, "Who is going to look after you? Do you have a good car? Did you eat? Are you tired?" Her concern for my well-being was unmistakable.

I usually waited until she fell asleep before leaving.

One night she asked me to sleep over. "You can sleep on the recliner." I said, "No thank you, I have to work in the morning." Another time she asked if I cooked at home. "I do when I have time," I said. Then she asked, "When will you be getting some time off from work?" I told her it would be soon.

She once told me, "You are a survivor." "Indeed, I am," I replied. She said that people can sense things and that it is not hurting anyone. I answered, "I can sense it, and I accept it."

As I was leaving one day, she hugged me and said, "You continue to do great things." I replied, "You made me great." Her words stayed with me, a reminder that those who shape us never stop believing in us.

The Morning I Walked Her Home

Another day, she had a bad cold. I called the care home and asked them to give her something and make sure she was covered up. The next day, I brought her cough drops.

Later, I learned from care workers that she asked about me when I was not around. She wanted to call me early in the morning. One nurse said she spoke about me and my mom at two in the morning. She told another worker, "Shelley was my favorite student. I cared for her when she was young."

She asked me if I still go to Hope, and I told her I don't go that often. Then she said she would like to visit there.

After a few days away, I returned. She asked, "Where have you been? I was a little concerned. I thought you flew the coop. I have your number. I was going to call you." I realized she feared I would leave and not come back.

One day, when I returned, she told me she had fallen. "My beautiful face," she said. One side was badly bruised, and I could see how much it hurt her. I bought her pillows to help ease the swelling.

Throughout our visits, I listened to her and reflected on her history. I came to understand that she had lived with significant losses. Perhaps my long absence had affected her as well. She had not known where I was or what had become of me.

We shared a bond unlike anything I had ever known, as if our souls had crossed paths in another lifetime. That is how powerful the connection was. At times, it even felt telepathic.

I returned because our story was not finished, and something deep inside me knew I had to come back.

Shelley Fraser

Chapter Forty
Her Final Days

October 31st was a day I had been looking forward to. I was eager to visit Sister John again, this time with a few different students. Dressed as a doctor for Halloween, I hoped the costume would surprise her and bring a little joy. We carried buckets of treats for the staff and a few special ones just for her.

When we arrived, I was startled to find her sitting in the common area in a wheelchair, something I had not seen before. In her room, her clothes were laid out, her suitcase sat on the bed, and several items had been removed from the closet. I wondered if she was being moved.

Sister John did not speak. I suspected she did not recognize me in costume, and she had not met these students before. But when I spoke, she began to look around. One student whispered, "I think she recognizes your voice." I sat across from her and kept talking, even though she remained silent. Then a student snapped a photo of us. My hand rested on her wheelchair armrest, and she gently placed hers over mine. It was a quiet, powerful moment of connection.

Concerned, I spoke with the nurse. She told me Sister John had a rough weekend and received last rites. Stunned, I promised I would return after school.

At the time, I was working on my Master of Education degree. One assignment asked us to write about a teacher who had deeply influenced us. The timing could not have been more perfect. I chose Sister John. The assignment focused on emotional intelligence and how a teacher shapes our lives. After receiving my professor's feedback, I compiled the essay into a blue binder with photos and short reflections from over the years. I planned to read it to her.

That Halloween evening, I returned. She was now in bed. Still in costume, I removed my makeup so she could truly see me. I sat beside her and said gently, "Sister, we are going to take this journey together," just as we had during other chapters of our lives. She did not respond, but I stayed close.

Then came the emotional part. I read my assignment, and the memories overwhelmed me. At one point, she rested her hand on her forehead. When I mentioned my mother, she let out a low groan. When I finished, she grabbed my arm and said, "I like your hair." I replied, "Thank you." Something in the story must have awakened a feeling in her, a memory. She wanted to connect.

It reminded me of Grade 7, when she had grabbed my arm in class. That night, she later asked for water or Pepsi, and I stayed with her until early morning to make sure she was okay.

I read the assignment to her on three separate occasions. Each time, it brought up emotions I had carried for years, and I hoped it brought her comfort too. A few days later, care workers told me she had eaten breakfast, watched TV, and seemed in good spirits. The bruise on her face from a recent fall was fading. They said she had had episodes before but often bounced back. I stayed hopeful, calling often, even while traveling to Calgary.

One day, when I took her hand and held it gently in mine, she whispered, "It hurts." In that small, trembling confession, I felt the weight of everything she had been carrying. She looked at me with tired eyes and asked, "Why does life have to be so miserable?" The question hung between us, heavy and unanswerable. After a moment, her expression shifted and she asked, "How are the boys?" meaning my brothers.

Another day, I arrived and found her dressed. I said, "I don't know if you know this, but I was here with you until early morning." She replied, "I don't remember that." I gave her ice water. She said, "It is nice and cold." Her ability to find something positive, even in decline, always amazed me. I covered her with blankets to keep her warm.

On a different afternoon, I sat quietly in her room. She asked, "Who are you." I said, "It's Shelley." She replied, "Shelley Fraser." I said yes. Then she said, "Shelley, get Father a cup of coffee," even though no one else was in the room. She asked, "Do you see that cute little girl?" Then she said, "I'm kind of hungry." I got her some toast. As I moved my jacket off the floor, she asked, "What are you doing?" I waited until she fell asleep before leaving.

As the days passed, her health declined. I didn't know how to help. I didn't want to overstep. I respected her choices, even when she refused food, but I worried. I brought her soup, sandwiches, pizza, and fruit. Sometimes she would eat a few bites, but it was not enough. She drank a little, but it could not sustain her.

One day, I arrived with tears in my eyes. I spoke to her, even though she had not said much lately. A care worker reassured me that she could still hear me. As I cried beside her, she looked at me and said, "Enough. I am sick." I replied gently, "I know you are." I wiped my tears. That moment stayed with me.

Another time, I saw a tear in her eye. It said everything. She whispered, "It won't be much longer now." I think she knew. Sometimes she would say, "I want to go home." This was not the life she wanted. She had endured enough.

Yet even in decline, her humor remained. If I was on the phone during visits, she would cough just enough to get my attention, a subtle reminder that I was there to be with her.

One evening, she asked me to help her up. I found someone to assist, and we wheeled her to the TV room. Later, she said, "Let's go to bed. I want to go to bed." Back in her room, she asked for a cloth to wash her face. I fetched one. Then she wanted to get up again. I said, "I will try. Please give me your hands." She placed them in mine. I tried to lift her but could not. She smiled and teased, "Why are you so dainty." I laughed and said, "Sister, it's dead weight. I can't get you up." We smiled at each other.

Later, while I was on the phone, I noticed her face cloth by my foot. She must have thrown it at me, and I laughed. Another night, she asked me to rub lotion on her itchy legs. As I did, she sighed and said, "It feels so good."

I often raised her bed to help her breathe and reminded staff to keep her side rails up so she would not fall.

Her birthday was approaching, December 8. I visited on the 7th, bringing a birthday card and one signed by my students. I also brought a cupcake, knowing she could not eat much. I asked, "Would you like a piece." She said yes, then changed her mind.

I stayed until the early hours of her birthday, read both cards, and wished her a happy birthday. When I was about to leave, I told her I would return soon. I didn't want to intrude if others wished to visit.

The staff noticed our connection. Some even thought we were related. I would say, "We are not." But maybe they saw something deeper, shared mannerisms or a mirrored closeness. I had known Sister John for years. One day at the care home, the manager said, "She is your person, isn't she?" and I answered, "Yes, she is." When you are close to someone, you begin to reflect on each other.

Still, there were struggles. Sometimes Sister John wanted to get up, but the care workers insisted she stay in bed. I worried that staying in bed too long would weaken her. I questioned the nurse, and she said, "We give her medication, morphine, every six hours." There was also a time when Sister John needed to be changed. I went to the care worker and told her. She replied, "I will change her after my break." That break lasted nearly two hours. Although I was not always happy with the care Sister John received, I kept those concerns to myself. But I could see her spirit fading. I shared my frustrations with Sister John privately. Watching someone you love slowly waste away is heartbreaking. I often left feeling helpless.

Before leaving, I would sometimes tell her, "I love you." People need to say it more often to their loved ones. I came from a home where love was rarely expressed.

I spent many late nights with Sister John, sometimes until early morning. I shared photos and stories with the staff, and I would become emotional at times. They often told me, "She is lucky to have you," and I would answer, "I was lucky to have her." No one completely understood our depth. It was difficult, but loving, how two women could shape each other and still hold deep affection after years apart.

I have come to believe that Sister John and I needed those private moments to heal each other. She healed me by letting me stay and allowing me to care for her. I had been afraid of rejection, but she never pushed me away. In those quiet moments, we created space for our most intimate feelings. They were necessary, and they were healing.

A few nights before she passed, the same woman I had once helped with her wool around her wheelchair, who had also been a nurse, said, "She is only existing." I replied, "I know, and I don't know how to help her." She suggested I get a sponge from the nurse to help Sister John drink. I did.

I brought cold water and sat beside her. "Sister, I am going to try to give you some water. You have not been drinking," I said. I was nervous, afraid she might reject my help, but she didn't. For two to three hours, I gently offered her water with the sponge. She swallowed. It was not much, but it meant everything. I told her she had very nice skin. I reminded her of a memory of her standing on the street in Hope with her arms folded while Bruce Springsteen's "Glory Days" played from the car as we drove down Main Street. It was emotional and beautiful. When she had had enough to drink, she raised her hand, and I stopped.

I noticed her wedding band had shifted from her left hand to her right, even though it had always been on the left before.

On the eve of Sister John's passing, I arrived with my computer, sat down, and gently took her hand in mine. I felt a spark when our hands connected, as if everything we had not said was suddenly understood. I held her hand for a few hours, the longest I had ever held it. Then I let go and told her, "I will be back shortly," wanting to speak with the nurse.

When I returned, I noticed her breathing had changed. I believe she was waiting for me. She did not want to pass alone, and I did not want her to. Some people pass without anyone present. Others wait for someone they love, someone whose nearness gives them permission to rest.

As I stood beside her bed, I shared a few ultimate thoughts. One was, "This is really going to hurt," and I sobbed. I knew I was about to lose someone who had helped me find myself. Then she was gone.

It was painful, but beautiful. I wouldn't have traded it for the world. I wanted to be with her, even if it meant giving up my holidays. That is how much she meant to me. God granted me that wish, and I am forever grateful.

There is no age limit when it comes to loving someone. That is what I learned through this experience. She left this world deeply loved and did not pass alone. She had someone who truly saw her and loved her for who she was. I saw her as a human being.

I loved Sister John enough to stay, to cry, to care, to feed her and help her drink, to advocate, and to be present when she passed. And she loved me enough to let me in, to let me help, and to hold space for our shared history. That kind of love does not need words. It lives in the quiet, in touch, in memory, and in the heart. In the early hours of that morning, she left a part of herself with me that I will never forget.

In this world, no one gets a free ride. We all experience loss. But it is important to dig in and be present because it often does not last.

Ironically, when Sister John passed, I noticed my large brown envelope on her end table. Inside was the letter I had written her and some photos. What struck me most was that she had written my name and phone number on it and drawn four stars above my name. It also happened to be exactly four months to the day since I had reunited with her, the very day she passed.

How could anyone predict such perfect timing?

The love we had for each other transcended labels. It was spiritual, emotional, and deeply human.

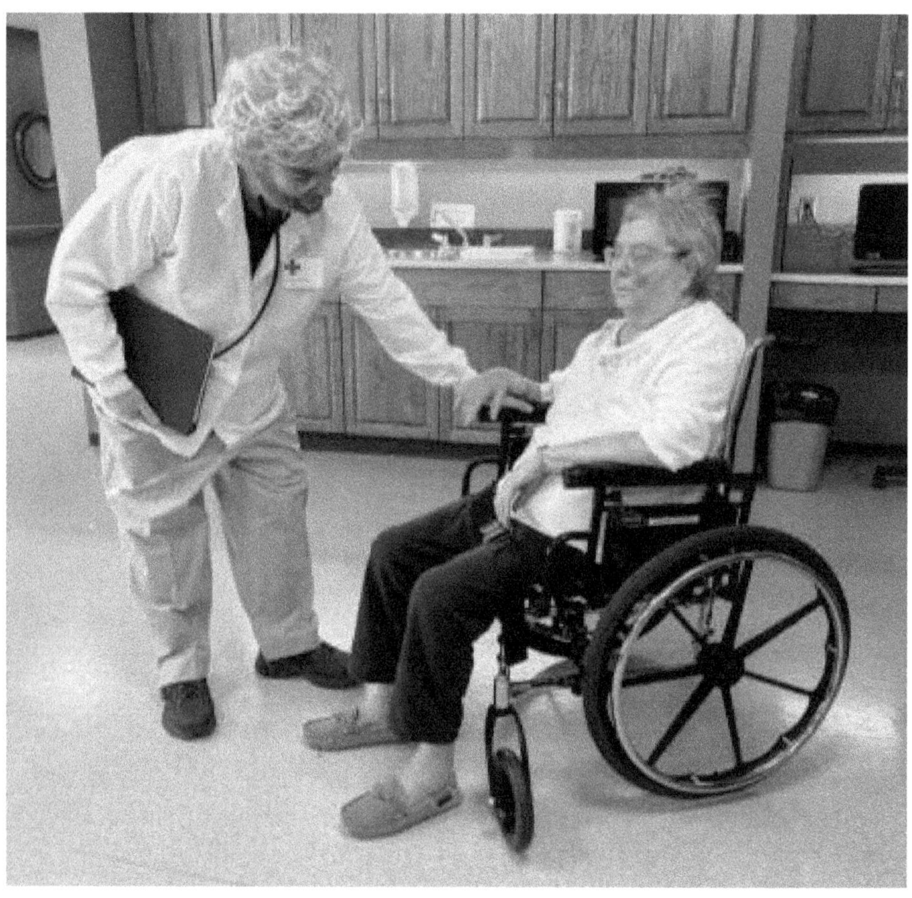

In 2024, Shelley dressed as a doctor for Halloween with Sister John. The photo captures the affection between them.

Shelley Fraser

Chapter Forty-One
She Probably Left with You

When Sister John passed away, I waited quietly for news of her funeral. One of her cousins, Sister Melissa, who is also a religious sister, kindly reached out to another cousin to make sure I was informed. I thought it was thoughtful of her to include me. I also gave Sister Melissa some sympathy cards to pass along to Sister John's family. Over the years, I had become friends with some of her relatives, though I never truly knew her brothers or sisters.

Before the funeral, I had quiet moments at home, grieving privately. I visited cousins and friends, spoke with my brothers, and surrounded myself with people who had known Sister John or met her at some point. Their support meant everything to me.

The day before the funeral, I contacted the funeral home and asked if I could spend some private time with her. I texted Emily, who replied that she would meet me there. I picked some roses for Sister John. When I entered the chapel, I saw her lying peacefully, alone. Emily and I placed the roses in a vase. I took one rose and gently sat it in her casket, along with a private letter I had written. Standing there felt surreal. Emotion washed over me as I realized it was truly over.

As I looked at her, memories flooded over me. I knew this day would come, but I could never have predicted how it would feel or how it would end. I leaned over and kissed her forehead, and as I did, I noticed her wedding ring still resting on her right finger. In that moment, I understood that those final months had brought healing to both of us. We had found peace, not just with each other but within ourselves. She had taught me what it meant to show up for someone, even when it was hard, and to love without expectation.

On the day of the funeral, a few of my students came with me. They wanted to be there for support. A few people from the Bounty Reserve also attended. I met and spoke with several of the sisters, telling some of them that I had been with Sister John when she passed. One of them thanked me for being there. I replied that I would have done anything for her. Some connections do not fit into categories. They simply exist, undeniable and unexplainable.

After the funeral, I went to the cemetery. I had a few quiet moments with Sister John and said, "Sister, let's get out of here." It was something she had once said to me in the care home. Then I continued to Calgary for the holidays. I played music and allowed myself to grieve in waves. I reflected on how fortunate I was to have been with her when she passed, and on all the years we had shared.

While in Calgary, I visited friends, and my brother and I attended midnight mass. Tears filled my eyes during the service. I thought about our long history. I was young when I first met Sister John, and over the decades our lives became deeply intertwined. There were challenges, both for her and for me.

But the truth is, we drew strength from each other in ways others might not understand. We filled something deep in each other that may have been missing in our own lives, and we found it in one another. It was a connection like no other. Loving her changed the shape of my life and losing her changed it again.

That is our history, and what a history it was. And it is not over, because a part of her still lives. Someone once said to me, "The day you left the care home after Sister John passed, she probably left with you." I laughed when I heard it, but deep down I knew exactly what they meant. And maybe she did. Love is what carries us forward. In the stillness that followed, I felt her presence more clearly than ever. In grief, signs of presence remind us that love transcends absence and continues to guide us.

The Morning I Walked Her Home

Shelley Fraser

Chapter Forty-Two
Synchronicities of Sister John

Since Sister John departed, life has been a time of adjustment. After her funeral, I was mentally and physically exhausted. I needed time to process my feelings. I already knew what it was like to be without her. I had experienced it before, but this time was different. She was now in spirit, no longer physically present.

I still had my education studies to complete and work to do. Staying motivated helped. It was a good distraction. But there were moments when I would sit in the kitchen and grieve. It was difficult to push through, yet I took it one day at a time. That was all I could do.

I had not given much thought to the afterlife until Sister John passed. Like many, I believed that once you are gone, that is it. But after speaking with others about their loved ones, they shared their experiences and encouraged me to stay open to the possibility. Slowly, I began noticing signs of my own. I knew some people might explain these moments differently, and I understood that, but for me they carried a meaning I could not ignore.

Shortly after she passed, I began finding dimes on the ground. During difficult moments, I would ask for guidance and often receive answers. Sometimes I would get emails from her relatives after especially emotional evenings. One time, while writing a letter to Sister John at the table, a Styrofoam bowl shook even though the table was solid. Other times, when visiting her cousin, I would feel a warmth so comforting that I would fall asleep. It felt like being wrapped in something unseen but deeply familiar.

The day before Emily's wedding, I received a rosary from Sister John's brother. The next day, at my student's wedding, I was deeply moved. After the service, I visited Sister John's grave. Later that evening, I found myself seated at a table with people I didn't know, each with some connection to her. One young lady's mother had worked with Sister John at the care home, and others had lived or worked at the

The Morning I Walked Her Home

"Big House" where she once resided. It felt like more than coincidence. The following day, I received an email from one of her relatives. It felt as though she was orchestrating something from beyond.

Another time at the cemetery, I noticed a headstone with a familiar last name and felt drawn to it. When I reached it, I saw Sister John's first name engraved. At a different cemetery, the same thing happened. I turned around and saw her first name again. It felt strange yet comforting.

Last winter, I went for a drive with one of her cousins. We ended up stuck on a gravel road with no clear path forward. I thought we were not getting out of that rut, but somehow, we did. I felt a push, and suddenly we were free. It felt like someone was helping us.

I truly felt Sister John was with me. When I completed my Master of Education degree, I received it in the seventh month, on the seventh day. I met Sister John in the seventh grade. Her care home room number was 7, and my parking stall was 7. Recently, I was assigned Box 7. I smiled when I saw it, subtle but unmistakable, like a quiet reminder that I was not alone.

After shoulder surgery this past summer, I did not need pain medication for five days, the longest I have ever gone without it. Another time, I had pain in my left leg, the one with blood clots. One morning, I prayed for relief. I felt warmth over my leg, and the pain disappeared. It was gentle but powerful.

I have had a few dreams, though not many. I was not much of a believer before, but I have had too many experiences to doubt that Sister John's presence is still around. I do not expect everyone to see these moments the way I do, but they bring me comfort and support my healing journey.

A friend named Sandy had never met Sister John, yet she told me she had a few dreams and shared what they were about. I listened closely. Even those who had not known her seemed to feel her presence.

Once, while speaking with my brother and his wife on the phone, we were talking about Sister John. I jokingly said, "If something strange happens, it is probably her." Shortly after, a photo on the wall partially came undone. I laughed, but I felt something deeper.

Another time, I was thinking aloud and said it would have been nice to have a photo of Sister John and me. Later, while looking through old emails she had sent while I was in Africa, I found a beautiful photo of the two of us. I have it hanging now. I feel she has her own way of coming through, not loudly or dramatically, but in ways only I would recognize.

We have to remember that Sister John and I were close for many years and that she was spiritual. As a religious sister, she likely had her own beliefs about the afterlife. As difficult as it has been at times, there continue to be many beautiful moments. I am sure she is still very much a part of them.

The Morning I Walked Her Home

Chapter Forty-Three
Give It Time

Grief and loss touch all of us in diverse ways. As human beings, we cannot escape them. At some point in our lives, we will experience loss, not only of people but also of careers, relationships, health, pets, or even parts of ourselves. Grief can come from divorce, someone moving away, the loss of a limb, or the onset of disability. How we process grief depends on many factors, including our perspective, emotional resilience, the support we have, and our outlook on life.

I learned grief young, and even then, I processed it differently. I believed in heaven, and that belief gave me comfort. As I grew older and lost both my parents, I realized I still had to live for myself and carry on. When I lost friends, I missed them deeply, but I came to understand they were in a better place, free from suffering. I still think of them now and then, but as time passes and new experiences unfold, the intensity of grief softens. They remain part of me, but the pain is no longer as sharp.

Pain is like a deep cut. It hurts and leaves a scar, but it heals. The scar may remain, and someone might ask how you got it. You choose whether to share that story. Grief is much the same. Losing someone or something important takes time, and the mark it leaves may never fully fade, but we learn to live with it. Over time, grief does not vanish. It reshapes itself into something we can carry.

No one grieves the same way. We must allow others the space they need to feel and heal in their own time. We cannot assume someone will be over it by now. We do not know the depth of their relationship or the strength of their attachment. Tears are not a sign of weakness. They are signs of healing. Grief often comes in waves. Some days it feels distant. Other days a song or memory brings tears. Grief does not move in a straight line. You can feel acceptance one day and sadness the next, and both are normal. Everyone grieves differently, and that is okay.

The Morning I Walked Her Home

While grief can consume us, it is important to remember those who are still with us. We must cherish the relationships we have now. I often tell students to stay present. One day we will all be together again, but for now, we have a purpose to fulfill.

When Sister John passed, I was overwhelmed with questions. How would I live without her? Could I have done more? Guilt crept in. I wondered if I should have returned sooner or cared for her differently. Guilt is one of the most common companions of grief, even when we have done everything we could. Then I realized that maybe she would have been miserable continuing in a life where she was ill and restricted. She could not go out and enjoy life. I wouldn't want her to remain unhappy.

I experienced the five stages of grief as described by Elisabeth Kübler-Ross in her book *On Death and Dying*. Denial surfaced first as I held onto hope that Sister John would recover. Bargaining followed as I gave more of myself, staying with her late into the night, bringing her food, and caring for her, but these efforts could not change the outcome. Anger then emerged as I felt frustration toward myself and others, questioning what more could have been done. Depression settled in as the reality of her decline became unavoidable, and I felt a deep sadness knowing that our time together was coming to an end. Eventually, I reached acceptance, recognizing that the decision was not mine to make. Her body was tired, and her spirit was ready.

In the end, I felt I had done everything humanly possible. If you feel you did all you could, that is all you can ask of yourself. What you feel after a loss is completely normal. We all experience different emotions, and they do not always appear in a particular order. Part of healing is learning to offer ourselves the same compassion we would offer a friend.

Sister John used to say, "Give it time." And she was right. New experiences came. New people entered my life. Laughter returned. I will never forget Sister John. I think of her every day, just as you think of your loved ones. Her memory is woven into the fabric of my life.

She is part of my story now, not only in remembrance but in how I live and love. The pain has softened, but the love remains.

Grief can hold you back if you let it. It can affect relationships and your ability to live fully. But we are here for a reason. Our loved ones shaped us, and their influence remains. Some people feel they have lost their person and will never be the same. Others accept that life is finite and embrace each moment. Everyone is on a different page when it comes to grief.

It is important to remember that you are alive today. The people around you are part of your journey. Make the most of it. Life is short. Wake up each day and challenge yourself to live it. It will not always be easy, and rough patches are part of the process. But believe in yourself. Reflect on your triumphs. They may help you, and they may help others.

Five months after Sister John passed, I started a Grief Share group at a Catholic church in Prince Albert. People came weekly to share their stories. It was healing. It reminded us we were not alone.

You do not need to start a group to help others. Just be present. Listen. You do not need answers. Sometimes all someone needs is to be heard. In that listening, healing begins.

Grief softens with time, but love endures. It is the thread that carries us forward. In the end, grief teaches us not only how to let go but how to hold on to what truly matters.

The Morning I Walked Her Home

This photo was taken by co-facilitator Kaylee Vance in Prince Albert after she and Shelley completed a 12-week grief and loss program in July 2025. The comment above is from a Facebook post Kaylee shared that same month and is included here with her permission.

Shelley Fraser

Chapter Forty-Four
Life's Lessons

Since the loss of Sister John, many beautiful moments have continued to bring joy. It is important to reflect on these and appreciate simple things with gratitude. Too often we rush through our days without truly acknowledging the gift of each one.

We wake up looking forward to the weekend and sometimes take life for granted.

Life is fragile. We are all placed on this earth for a purpose. Whether that purpose unfolds over a short or long time, we cannot predict it. Life can change or be taken in an instant.

That is why it is essential to remain present, not dwell too much on the past, and not worry excessively about the future. Presence is one of the greatest gifts we can give ourselves.

Many people live with regrets. I am sure Sister John did too, and so have I. But when people know their time may be ending, they often find the strength to overlook their shortcomings.

None of us are perfect. We have all made mistakes. Grace lives in the choice to keep going and to keep growing.

What matters is how we choose to live now. I have chosen to live in the present because what happens today becomes tomorrow's past.

When life feels overwhelming, living one day at a time is a powerful way to stay grounded. It reminds us that we do not need to solve everything at once.

Revisiting the past can be comforting if it brings good memories. But if it drags us down, it may not be worth revisiting. That is where depression can quietly sneak in and remind us that we have lost touch with ourselves. Painful experiences can be set aside, understood as lessons, and used to prepare us for future challenges. Every experience teaches us something, and each lesson is unique to our journey.

Shelley Fraser

Sometimes the hardest lessons become the ones that shape us most. Growth often comes from places we never expected.

Reflecting on the lessons life has offered me, I recognize the role one extraordinary woman played in my early understanding of grief, healing, and purpose. Her influence is part of my story, but the path that followed became my own.

These lessons bring me back to Sister John, whose legacy remains an important part of my journey. Her presence shaped the beginning of my understanding, and the meaning continues to unfold as I move forward.

The Morning I Walked Her Home

Chapter Forty-Five
The Quiet Grace of Two Lives

As I near the end of this memoir, I find myself reflecting not only on Sister John's life but on my own. What began as the story of a Catholic sister and a young girl became a journey of healing, rediscovery, and personal transformation.

Sister John was not just a chapter in my life. She was a turning point. Her presence challenged me, comforted me, and ultimately changed me. Through her, I learned that meaningful relationships do not always follow a script. They do not need to be explained to be real.

There were times when I did not know how to move forward, times I questioned whether I belonged in her world or she in mine. But somehow, we found our way back to one another. In her final months, there was peace, clarity, and a sense of understanding that stayed with me long after she was gone.

It has been over a year since Sister John's passing, and in that time, I have come to see her life with greater clarity. She lived with a profound duality, one life devoted to her vocation and service, and another carried quietly, shaped by personal challenges and the depth of her inner world.

Carrying the weight of that private life must have been difficult, yet it revealed her humanity. Though she kept much from the world, those close to her knew the sincerity of her heart. I came to understand aspects of her life that were not always visible to others, and I valued the trust she placed in me.

With time, I understood how deeply she cared for the people in her life, including me. Out of respect for her, I accepted the quiet nature of that care, knowing she was guided by the responsibilities of her vocation.

Today, I remember Sister John not only for her devotion and service but also for the steadiness with which she carried her burdens. Her life was complex, her compassion was genuine, and her memory remains a blessing. Letting go was difficult for many of us because meaningful connections leave a lasting imprint.

Over the years, I visited Sister John in twelve different places, a few of which she returned to, each holding its own memory. Though our relationship had its challenges, it shaped me in ways I continue to recognize. Life with the religious is never simple. Their vows guide them, yet they remain human. We learned from each other, sometimes through difficulty and sometimes through joy. Sister John was remarkable. What endures is not the struggle but the quiet grace of two lives that intersected in meaningful ways.

This memoir is not just a tribute to her. It is a reminder that every life we touch leaves a mark. That care, when offered sincerely, continues long after we are gone. That grief reflects the depth of our connections. And that healing is possible, even when the heart feels heavy.

I gave Sister John what I could. I gave her my time, my trust, and my presence. I offered companionship when she needed support, comfort when she faced challenges, and laughter when the days felt heavy. I ensured she was remembered not just as a sister but as a woman who contributed deeply to the lives around her.

More than anything, I carry gratitude for what she taught me. In return, she gave me confidence, perspective, and a renewed sense of purpose.

If you have walked this journey with me, thank you. If you have grieved, I hope you have found comfort. If you have cared deeply for someone, I hope you have seen yourself in these pages. And if you are still searching for meaning, I hope you know it is okay to take your time.

Time does not erase the pain, but it softens it. It makes room for joy again. It reminds us that life continues to unfold, and that we continue to grow. In the quiet spaces between loss and renewal, we learn that healing is not a single moment but a steady becoming. And in that becoming, we find our way forward.

Shelley Fraser

Chapter Forty-Six
The Legacy of Sister John

I will always remember Sister John. She became a profound part of my life and shaped me in ways I never could have imagined. Her love and care gave me the strength to believe I could do better, and I did. Without her guidance, I truly don't know where I would be today.

As I have said before, we both took a risk. I did when I opened my heart to a Catholic sister, and she did when she embraced someone from a complicated background. But no one walks through life alone. We shaped each other. In the end, I did not return to her because of our past. I returned because she mattered. She never forgot me. She wondered where I had gone when I disappeared. She never asked for anything in return. I wanted to be there for her because I loved her. It was not obligation. It was devotion.

To honor her legacy, I had a memorial bench created in her memory. She deserved it. I felt her name needed to return to her family plot so others could see that she was not only a religious figure but an extraordinary human being. It is an uncommon honor for a Catholic sister. I am deeply grateful to Sister John's family for allowing me to honor her, and to the cemetery crew and parish of Jackson Lake for making it possible. I know she would be laughing about it, but I also know she would feel honored.

Before she passed, we spoke about where she would be buried. She told me she would be laid to rest with the sisters in Prince Albert. I often visit her there. I have quiet moments talking to her, reflecting on our memories, and asking for guidance. Sometimes I leave her a rose. It is still hard to accept that she is gone, but I can still feel her presence. How could I not? She is in silence, the memories, and in the way I still speak her name.

One day, I happened to be reading her cousin's family history book. In it, I found Sister John's write-up. She mentioned her formative and high school education, the year she entered the novitiate, when she made her final profession, and her university studies. She also described her teaching career, noting that she taught for many years, mainly junior high and high school, and spent five years teaching in another province.

What struck me most was what she chose to highlight. When discussing her teaching years, she specifically mentioned 1986, when she taught in Hope, my home community, and later how much she enjoyed working at the Bounty Reserve, where I worked alongside her for many years. She did not mention any other schools from her long career, only those two places that held such meaning for both of us.

That felt meaningful. Clearly, those places held significance for her. Knowing that created a deeper sense of connection to her story. It was a quiet reminder that the time we shared had value in both of our lives.

True legacy lives not in titles but in the impact, we leave behind. Remembering Sister John reminds me that grief is not just a personal experience. It is something we all encounter in our own way. Her loss opened my heart to a deeper understanding of how we mourn, how we heal, and how we carry the memory of those we have cared for. And to anyone finding their way through grief, I hope you know you are not walking alone.

The Morning I Walked Her Home

196

Chapter Forty-Seven
To Those Who Grieve

Grief is a deeply personal journey. While the pain may feel overwhelming now, with time it will soften. Be gentle with yourself. Allow space for your emotions. Let the tears come when they need to. Take a quiet drive, sit in prayer, talk to someone you trust, or visit a place that brings you peace. What you are feeling is normal.

If possible, try to avoid numbing the pain with alcohol or substances. They may offer temporary relief, but they often deepen the hurt and delay healing. Sadness, confusion, anger, guilt, or even brief moments of peace are all part of the natural process of bereavement.

Some days will feel heavier than others. Grief changes shape as time passes. It may feel sharp one day and quieter the next. There is no shame in the ebb and flow of emotion. It is simply the heart learning how to carry what it cannot change.

Do not be hard on yourself. There is no right way to grieve and no timeline you must follow. Healing is not about forgetting. It is about learning to carry love forward, even in absence. You are allowed to feel, to fall, to rest, and to rise again. Each step is part of your healing.

Above all, remember you are not alone. There are people who care, even when you feel isolated. Let them in when you are ready. Grief is the price of love, and healing begins when we allow ourselves to feel and to be heard.

Grief connects us, but so does love, the kind that shapes us long before loss ever arrives. As I continued to reflect on my own journey, I found myself returning to the quiet and powerful bond that defined so much of my life. It is in that space between love and loss that the quiet grace of two intertwined lives becomes clear.

The Morning I Walked Her Home

Chapter Forty-Eight
Where the Heart Finally Speaks

In the end, life is a journey of connection, growth, and meaning. The people who walk beside us, whether briefly or for many years, help shape who we become. Sister John was one of those rare souls whose presence leaves an imprint that time cannot erase. Our bond endured across years and distance because something genuine kept drawing us back to one another.

Writing this story was difficult and often deeply emotional. It required me to return to memories I had spent years trying to understand. For a long time, I did not realize that Sister John had been trying to express her feelings, and I had not been able to meet her in that space. I felt too vulnerable and too afraid to acknowledge what she might have been trying to tell me, especially given her vocation and the identity she carried. Others saw what I could not face, and perhaps that is why I struggled so much. Recognizing her humanity would have meant confronting my own.

During those months at the care home, something shifted. I finally found the courage to say to her, "I think I finally understand, Sister."

Speaking truth to someone you love is never easy, but silence becomes its own kind of loss. Once a person is gone, the words you held back remain forever unspoken. Those four months gave us a small window, and in that space, we found clarity, tenderness, and truth. I was finally able to acknowledge my feelings, and in doing so I realized they had been mutual all along. There had always been unmistakable energy between us, a quiet chemistry that shaped every moment we shared.

I carry her with me as I move forward, living with intention and welcoming each day as a gift. Near the end of her life, she told me, "You're the one." She meant that I had truly seen her, understood her, and walked beside her in a way that mattered. Our connection shaped her life as deeply as she shaped mine. I once told her I might share our story because it was so unique and fascinating, and as I finish these reflections, I realize I have kept that promise.

Her life taught me that even in loss there is meaning. Love does not disappear. It changes form. In that transformation we find the strength to continue, to grow, and to love again. Letting go is never simple, but it often brings unexpected peace.

The journey Sister John and I shared was extraordinary, an experience whose influence will remain with me always. We both carried our sufferings quietly, and in that quiet endurance we discovered something rare. The challenges we faced did not diminish us. They revealed who we were. In facing what was difficult, I came to understand the strength that had been forming within me all along.

I never imagined I would be with Sister John as she took her final breath. If I had told her twenty or thirty years earlier that I would be with her at the end of her life, I don't think she would have believed it, and neither could I have imagined finding myself in such a position. Yet life has its way of bringing us back to the people who need us most. It was a gift for both of us.

Emily came into my life at exactly the right moment. Through her, I found my way back to someone who had shaped me more than I ever realized. My relationship with Sister John was one of the most difficult I ever experienced, yet also one of the most rewarding. Being with her as she left this world was one of the greatest honors of my life, and at the same time it opened something within me. I finally understood the depth of what we shared, even though our lives unfolded in ways that kept those feelings quiet and unspoken until the very end.

As I close this memoir, I think of the song that captures the spirit of our story, "Wind Beneath My Wings," made famous by Bette Midler. Its message of gratitude and quiet strength reflects the way Sister John lifted my life in ways I did not always recognize.

And so, I move forward carrying what she gave me, forever grateful for the love and care that shaped my life.

Shelley Fraser

About the Author

Shelley Fraser is a Canadian author with Métis heritage, a Licensed Professional Counsellor, and a recipient of the Saskatchewan Volunteer Award for Outstanding Volunteerism. She holds an MEd in leadership. Shelley has taught mental health at the post-secondary level, supported newcomers to Canada, and served in leadership roles across education and community service. She credits Indigenous communities for shaping her understanding of healing, resilience, and wisdom, lessons that continue to guide her work and her writing.

She is the author of several self-published titles, including *Broken Trust*, *New Beginnings*, *Unexpected Guests*, and *Right from the Heart*. Yet none of her previous books prepared her for the story she tells here, the one she carried quietly for decades.

This memoir is a tribute to Sister John, the Catholic sister who stepped into Shelley's life when she was a vulnerable young girl and offered the stability, guidance, and love she had never known. Their bond stretched across forty-four years and survived distance, silence, and the unpredictable turns of life. After more than a decade apart, they found their way back to each other only four months before Sister John's passing, a reunion that proved love, once given, never truly disappears.

This is the story of two women whose connection rose above time and circumstance. One was nearing the end of her journey in a care home, and the other was building a life devoted to helping others heal. Their relationship, marked by courage, grace, and devotion, helped shape Shelley into the woman she is today.

Shelley sitting on Sister John's memorial bench, 2025.

The Morning I Walked Her Home